Using your *Spiritual* GIFTS

EQUIPPED TO SERVE. ENGAGED IN SERVING.

Using your Spiritual GIFTS

EQUIPPED TO SERVE. ENGAGED IN SERVING.

EDDIE RASNAKE

Advancing the Ministries of the Gospel

AMG *Publishers*

God's Word to you is our highest calling.

Using Your Spiritual Gifts

© 2004 by Eddie Rasnake

Published by AMG Publishers. All Rights Reserved.

Fifth Printing, 2007

ISBN 10: 0-89957-277-4
ISBN 13: 978-089957277-2

Cover design by Jeanie Tillman
at ImageWright Marketing and Design, Chattanooga, TN (www.imagewright.net)

Editing and interior layout by Rick Steele

Printed in Canada
12 11 10 09 08 07 –T– 10 9 8 7 6 5

This book is dedicated to

John Meador

I know of no one who more clearly possesses the gift of leadership. His vision and leading made this project become a reality, and his friendship made it fun.

Acknowledgments

I am ever grateful to my dear friends, Wayne Barber and Rick Shepherd, with whom I partnered in the conception of this Bible study series that became "Following God." A big thank you to the folks at AMG Publishers for their high view of the Word of God and their commitment to quality, accuracy, and depth in all the Bible study resources they produce. I am grateful to partner with a publisher that places the ministry side of writing as more important than the business side. Special kudos to Rick Steele, Trevor Overcash, Dale Anderson, and Dan Penwell for their help and support. Special thanks as well to the people of Woodland Park Baptist Church for whom this material was originally developed. Most of all, I remain grateful to the Lord Jesus, who saved a wretch like me and continues to lead me in what it means to follow Him with a whole heart.

EDDIE RASNAKE

About the Author

Eddie Rasnake met Christ in 1976 as a freshman in college. He graduated with honors from East Tennessee State University in 1980. He and his wife, Michele, served for nearly seven years on the staff of Campus Crusade for Christ. Their first assignment was the University of Virginia, and while there they also started a Campus Crusade ministry at James Madison University. Eddie then served four years as campus director of the Campus Crusade ministry at the University of Tennessee. In 1989, Eddie left Campus Crusade to join Wayne Barber at Woodland Park Baptist Church as the Associate Pastor of Discipleship and Training. He has been ministering in Eastern Europe in the role of equipping local believers for more than a decade and has published materials in Albanian, German, Greek, Italian, Romanian, and Russian. Eddie serves on the boards of directors of the Center for Christian Leadership in Tirana, Albania, and the Bible Training Center in Eleuthera, Bahamas. He also serves as chaplain for the Chattanooga Lookouts (Cincinnati Reds AA affiliate) baseball team. Eddie and his wife Michele live in Chattanooga, Tennessee with their four children.

About the Following God Series

Three authors and fellow ministers, Wayne Barber, Eddie Rasnake, and Rick Shepherd, teamed up in 1998 to write a character-based Bible study for AMG Publishers. Their collaboration developed into the title, *Life Principles from the Old Testament*. Since 1998 these same authors and AMG Publishers have produced five more character-based studies—each consisting of twelve lessons geared around a five-day study of a particular Bible personality. More studies of this type are in the works. Two unique titles were added to the series in 2001: *Life Principles for Worship from the Tabernacle* and *Living God's Will*. These titles became the first Following God™ studies to be published in a topically-based format (rather than character-based). However, the interactive study format that readers have come to love remains constant with each new Following God™ release. As new titles are being planned, our focus remains the same: to provide excellent Bible study materials that point people to God's Word in ways that allow them to apply truths to their own lives. More information on this groundbreaking series can be found on the following web page:

www.amgpublishers.com

Preface

Every believer has at least one spiritual gift. I can say that confidently because God's Word states that emphatically. And God wants every believer to put their giftedness to use for the benefit of others. Peter wrote, *"As each one has received a special gift, employ it in serving one another as good stewards of the manifold grace of God"* (1 Peter 4:10). But after more than twenty years in vocational ministry I am amazed at how few people even know what their gifts are, let alone are putting them into service. It ought not be this way!

The Protestant Reformation was birthed by great men like Martin Luther, who believed that the Word of God should be the final authority for our faith and that God's Word was not meant to be the sole passion of the clergy. As a result of Luther's leadership, passion, courage, and sacrifice, the Bible was translated into the language of the common man, and Scripture was put into the hands of the people. I am so grateful for this blessing, and I am convinced that it is right. But the job is not finished. I believe there is a need for a second reformation. In the same way that Scripture was taken away from being the sole possession of the clergy and put into the hands of the laity, there is a need for a similar transfer with the work of ministry. The world will not be reached with only the paid professionals engaged in service. God wants to involve all of us uniquely and individually in the harvest fields of ministry. If we are the body of Christ, then it takes all of us for Him to be manifest today.

This book was created to be a resource to help move people out of the pews and into the harvest fields. My prayer is that you will find it helpful.

Yours and His,

Eddie Rasnake

EDDIE RASNAKE

Table of Contents

Producing Fruit

In East Tennessee, where I grew up, each season has its own distinct beauty, but fall is the most inspiring. Each autumn, the mountains are painted like fireworks as the leaves turn from summer's green to fluorescent shades of red, yellow, and orange. The splendor of the autumn season in this part of the country is truly spectacular to behold! From the deep reds of the oaks, to the brilliant oranges of the poplar trees, to the many shades and hues of the maples, God has displayed His splendor in a special way during this season. I'm not what you would call an expert when it comes to trees, but I do know some of their names. I know an apple tree, because I can see the apples hanging on it. The same is true for peach, pear, and cherry trees. I know oaks by their acorns and walnut and hickory trees by the nuts they produce. I know dogwood trees by their blossoms in spring and berries in fall. I know maples by the helicopter seeds they bear each fall, and I can even spot some trees by the shape of their leaves. But I would be hard-pressed to identify many at all in the winter when the branches are bare. I just love to spend time in the woods though, and over the years I've learned a thing or two from them. One thing I have learned is that it is the fruit which the tree bears that helps me to identify it.

"Each tree is known by its own fruit. . . ."
Luke 6:44

In John 15, Jesus tells the parable of the vine and the branches. He emphasizes in this passage that we are to "abide" in Him as the branches "abide" or stay connected to the vine. However, if we focus solely on abiding, we might miss the end result. The Bible says that the result of our fellowship with God will be manifested as "fruit." He will produce visible markers in our lives that identify us as His children. It was said of some of Jesus' disciples, *"Now as they observed the confidence of Peter and John and understood that they were uneducated and untrained men, they were amazed, and began to recognize them as having been with Jesus"* (Acts 4:13). Can it be said of those around us that we are followers of Jesus? Do others see a difference in our lives? That is what God desires. He wants to bear His fruit through us. And not just a little bit—He wants to bear "much fruit" in us (John 15:8).

WHAT IS FRUIT?

When Jesus says He wants to bear fruit in us (John 15:8), He uses the word "fruit" to signify the visible evidence of His work in us. But I think He implies more than just that. Picturing fruit leads your mind to conjure up images of delicious things. I think of tart, crunchy apples or sweet, juicy peaches. You see, our lives should not only bear evidence of God, but that evidence should be attractive and beneficial to others. God created each of us to be a blessing to others. He wants to work in us, so that He can work through us in ways that minister. Ministry isn't just something reserved for the clergy. God wants every Christian to have a ministry. In John 15:7–8, Jesus said that one sign that proves we are His disciples is that we bear much fruit. He also says in Luke 22:27, *"I am among you as one who serves."* Think about that. Did He serve us only so we could sit back and be served? NO! If God's plan for us is to become like Christ, then maturing will always mean serving. We won't all serve the same way, but every mature believer will have a ministry of some kind. Everyone will bear fruit.

📖 Read John 15:16.

What does it mean to be "appointed"?

_____

_____

_____

_____

For what purpose are we appointed as believers?

_____

_____

_____

_____

_____

What do you think it means that our fruit should "remain"?

_____

_____

_____

_____

While the words of John 15 are spoken directly to Jesus' original disciples, indirectly they speak to every follower of Jesus. Jesus reminds us that He chose us and appointed us for a specific purpose—that we should *"go and bear fruit."* To be appointed indicates that it is not our choice whether we will serve or not. It is our assignment to serve. We are called to "go," indicating that it is not merely a passive assignment, and we are called to "bear," indicating that we carry that which God produces in and through us. Finally, God desires that our fruit would be lasting. He doesn't want us to be a "flash in the pan," but He wants us to endure and make a lasting difference.

What is spiritual fruit? We know what apples, oranges, peaches, and bananas are. We easily recognize physical fruit. But what is "fruit" in a spiritual sense? If we are to bear fruit, we ought to have an understanding of what it is. Today, we want to look at a number of different passages in the Bible that use this word "fruit" and see what it is and what it is not.

📖 What do the following verses teach us about spiritual fruit?

Galatians 5:22–23

_____

_____

_____

_____

Matthew 3:8

_____

_____

_____

Ephesians 5:8–10

_____

_____

_____

_____

Do these verses share any common ground?

_____

_____

_____

Did You Know?
? **FRUIT OF THE SPIRIT**

Galatians 5:22–23 lists nine character qualities, but it speaks of them as the "fruit" of the Spirit, not the "fruits." Some commentators believe this singular reference means that the "fruit of the Spirit" is love, which is mentioned first. The other qualities expand on this and reveal the many different ways love manifests itself.

Think about what we learn here. The fruit mentioned in Galatians 5:22–23 are the character qualities produced in us as we abide with Christ—love, joy, peace, patience, kindness, goodness, faithfulness, gentleness, and self-control. What attractive people we become when Christ produces His character in us! In Matthew 3:8, Jesus speaks of bearing fruit *"in keeping with repentance."* This indicates that a contrite and repentant heart about sin is one of the evidences of God working in us. Ephesians 5:8–10 tells us that we are to *"walk as children of light."* The fruit of such a walk is expressed in *"all goodness and righteousness and truth."* If God is at work in us, He will produce that which is good, right, and true. The commonality we see in each of these passages is a change in character.

What do the following verses teach about biblical "fruit?"

Romans 1:13

_____

_____

_____

Romans 15:28

_____

_____

_____

Colossians 1:10

_____

_____

_____

Do these verses share any common ground?

_____

_____

_____

_____

_____

Not only does Jesus work changes in our character, but He also works through us to benefit others. In Romans 1:13, Paul seems to use the word "fruit" to mean ministry results along the lines of evangelism and discipleship. Looking at Romans 15:28, one can see that the word "fruit" refers to the results of the believers' walk with God, which, in this case, was an offering for impoverished believers in Jerusalem from the Christians in Macedonia and Achaia (the churches of Thessalonica, Phillipi, Berea, and Corinth, as well as others). In Colossians 1:10 fruit is again linked with good works. The common thread in each of these passages is that as a result of God's work in our character, He desires to do a work in our communities as well—working through us in ministry what He has worked in us in maturity.

Who Is Supposed to Bear Fruit?

Who is the minister at your church? Think before you answer that question, because how you answer it is very important. How your church answers this question is equally as important. Sadly, the mind-set of many churches is that the clergy are the ministers and the congregations are applauding spectators. Church life in a lot of places is much like a sporting event, where you have a handful of people in the action in desperate need of rest being cheered on by thousands in the stands in desperate need of exercise. But is that how God sees it? NO! The Scriptures make it very clear that God wants each of us to be a minister. Think about it. God wants each of us to live lives of spiritual fruitfulness. He wants to so work in us that He is able to work through us to the benefit of others.

📖 Look at Ephesians 2:10. According to this verse, what should be the outcome of a relationship with God?

_____

_____

_____

_____

Ephesians 2:8–9 are incredibly familiar verses to many of us. We are saved by grace, not works. But often the message of verse 10 is omitted. We are not saved **by** works, but we are saved **for** works. *"We are His workmanship."* If we were saved by our own works, we would be our own workmanship, but we are saved as a result of His work. But the outcome of His working in us ought to be His working through us. Another subtle message here is that our works are "prepared beforehand." In other words, God already has a plan for how He wants to use us. It isn't a matter of us simply being busy; we must be busy about the things God has for us personally. God has a plan for each life that is unique and significant!

📖 Read 1 Peter 4:10–11.

What does this passage say *"each one"* has received?

_____

_____

_____

What are they to do with what they have received?

_____

_____

_____

What different ways can we minister according to these verses?

_____

_____

_____

> *"As each one has received a special gift, employ it in serving one another, as good stewards of the manifold grace of God."*
>
> *I Peter 4:10*

This passage makes a powerful statement to all Christians. It tells us that **each one** of us has received a *"special gift."* These verses don't go into great detail about what that gift is, but we do know what we are to do with it—we are to employ it (put it to work) in serving others. In fact, it tells us that when we do, we are being good stewards of that gift. The next verse presents two categories of gifts: speaking gifts and serving gifts. Whatever we do in service, God should be glorified in it.

The gifts Peter writes about are what we call "spiritual gifts." Every Christian has been given at least one, but none of us (except Jesus) has all of them. If you think about it, these truths make two guarantees:

1) Knowing that each of us has at least one gift assures us that **the Church needs us.** It won't be all it could be without what we have to offer.

2) Knowing that no one has all the gifts makes certain that **we need the Church.** We need what others have to give. God has designed the body of Christ (the Church) in such a way as to guarantee interdependence.

📖 Look at Romans 12:1–6a. What must happen first before we can know God's will for our lives? (12:1–2)

_____

_____

_____

How do verses 3–5 explain that God has made the Church?

_____

_____

_____

What are we to do with our gifts? (verse 6a)

_____

_____

_____

_____

Word Study
GRACE GIFTS

The Greek word for "grace" (*charis*) is also the root of the word for spiritual gifts (*charisma*). The suffix *ma* in Greek means "the results of," and *charisma* means "the results of grace." We did nothing to earn our spiritual giftedness, nor can we change it by self-effort. It is a result of God's grace.

Before we can know God's will for our lives, we must first put ourselves at His disposal. We must offer ourselves to be used by Him. Once we are willing to be used, He will show us His good, acceptable, and perfect will for when, where, and how. In verses 3–5, we clearly see several important truths: **a)** God has given each of us a measure of faith; **b)** the Church is like the human body with many different parts; **c)** the parts of the body don't all have the same function. Verses 6–8 begin to show us some of those differences. This passage lists seven different spiritual gifts—grace endowments for service—that enable us to be useful in the Church and the Church's mission. Each of us has one of these gifts, but none of us have all of them. Whichever gift God has given us in His grace, we are to exercise it in the body. You see, we did nothing to earn these spiritual gifts since they are given by God's grace. Neither can we change our giftedness by our own efforts. Our giftedness comes only by God's sovereign choice.

If you don't know what your spiritual gift is, don't worry. You don't have to figure it out right away—we'll be studying this subject for the next twelve weeks. But beyond that, you will be studying this subject the rest of your Christian life. As you seek to serve the Lord as He gives opportunity, your own giftedness will become evident over time. It isn't just what you do; it is a part of who you are. It will manifest itself in the kinds of service you enjoy, the types of serving you do that God blesses, the serving others affirm about you, and the opportunities God gives you. When you are serving in your giftedness it will energize you—not drain you. And when you serve in your giftedness, others will benefit. The main things you need to understand are that God wants to use you and He has made you useable. Every Christian is supposed to bear fruit.

HOW DOES GOD WANT TO USE US?

Have you ever thought about why you are here on Planet Earth? If heaven is the very best place for the Christian, then why aren't we there already? Since God is all-powerful, it would be a simple thing for Him to take us there. Why don't we go straight to heaven when we become Christians? Why do we have to stay down here in a fallen world, waging war with sin and temptation? Why do we stay here struggling with sickness, aging, and death? If heaven is the place with no tears, no death, no pain, and no sin, why are we here? The answer to all these questions is that God has a purpose for the rest of our time on Planet Earth—and it isn't to make money. God leaves us here because He wants others to come to know His love and mercy through our witness. God's ultimate best is for us to be with Him in heaven, but right now, He has something planned for us that is equally important. He wants to work through us on earth so that others can join us in eternity.

📖 The apostle Paul seemed to be debating these very questions in his letter to the church at Philippi. Read Philippians 1:21–25 and write down what you learn.

_____

_____

_____

_____

_____

_____

Paul wrote this letter to Philippi from prison, and he seemed to be debating whether or not he would get out of there alive. In this consideration, he gives us a good list of the benefits both of living and of dying. To die, he says, is gain. In verse 23 he calls it *"very much better."* Yet he also recognized that to live would mean fruitful labor (verse 22). Getting specific as to what that labor would be in verse 25, he states that his living on and serving Christ would result in the joy and progress in the faith of others. To be in heaven would be better, but to remain on earth for a time is necessary. It is our remaining that allows us to minister to others.

Word Study
TO LIVE IS CHRIST

In the Greek language there are two different words for life: *bios* (from which we get our term, biology—study of life in general) and *zoē* (from which we get our term, zoology—study of higher life forms). It is this second word the apostle Paul uses here. *Zoē* generally connotes quality of life as opposed to mere existence. This is the word Jesus used in John 10:10 when He said, *"I have come that they might have life"*—not just mere existence, but a higher quality of life. When Paul says, *"to live is Christ,"* he means to really live, not just to exist.

📖 Look at 2 Corinthians 5:19–21.

Since Christ died for us, what should be our appropriate response (verse 15)?

_____

_____

_____

What did God do with us after He reconciled us to Himself through Christ (verses 18–19)?

_____

_____

_____

What ideas are communicated that we are God's ambassadors (verse 20)?

_____

_____

_____

Christ died for us to free us from the burden of sin, not so that we could continue to wallow in it. He died for us to free us from selfish living. He liberated us so we could live for Him instead of for ourselves. Part of that living is woven into the ministry of reconciliation He has given to us. He wants to use us to help others be reconciled to Him. In fact, Christ has made us His ambassadors. Think about that. An ambassador is someone who lives in a foreign country so that he can represent his home country there. Not living for himself, but for the one he represents, he speaks the words and wishes of his native land to a foreign government. In the same way, Earth is not our home. It is the assignment of our ambassadorship. It is the place we serve on behalf of the place that truly is our home—heaven.

One of the ways God wants to minister through us is by us representing Him to those who don't know Him. But there is more.

📖 Look at Matthew 28:18–20. What else does God want us to do?

_____

_____

_____

_____

God has given us the task of making disciples of all the nations. This task does not merely encompass evangelism. Conversion is not enough. God wants people to be made into disciples or followers of Him. He wants them to observe His commands and to identify with Him and His people. He wants each of us to help with that.

Biblical fruit involves us becoming more like Christ in our character, and as a result, we are to participate in His work—the work of evangelism and discipleship. Now, each one of us will not do this in exactly the same way. Our giftedness comes into play here.

Earth is not our home. It is the place we serve on behalf of the place that truly is our home— heaven.

Have you ever thought about the role spiritual giftedness plays in evangelism? We know that Ephesians 4 mentions *"evangelist"* as one of the positions of church leadership. Does this mean that some are gifted for evangelism and the rest of us keep quiet? Certainly not! Jesus makes it clear in Acts 1:8 that one of the results of the Spirit coming is that we would all be His witnesses. Giftedness does not determine if we will share Christ; all are called to that. What giftedness determines is how we will gain the opportunity to share Christ. Think of your spiritual gift as the key that opens the door for you to share. If you are gifted with mercy, then most often it will be your showing of mercy that makes the unbeliever open to hear what you have to say about Christ. If you are gifted with service, then it will often be your serving that makes others want to listen to what you have to say. If you are gifted with giving, then giving will be a key that opens doors to the gospel. Whatever your giftedness is, most often that is the very thing that will provide you with opportunities to share Christ. I have led more people to Christ while simply teaching the Scriptures in a group setting than I have through one-on-one evangelism. It is through the exercise of our giftedness that God enables us to share Christ. What is your giftedness? That is where you need to look for opportunities to share the gospel! That is how God wants to bear fruit through you.

The Motive of Reward

While we consider this idea that God wants every Christian to "bear fruit" or to engage in some kind of ministry, one further consideration should be mentioned: our service will be rewarded. At first glance, it sounds kind of unspiritual to hold out the carrot of reward as a motivation for serving Christ. After all, shouldn't the love of Christ alone compel us to want to serve Him? Isn't using reward as a motive simply promoting a selfish view of service, "I'm in it for what I get out of it"? John 10 contrasts the good shepherd (who truly cares for his sheep) with the hireling (the one who tends them only to get a paycheck). It is true that the heartbeat of ministry cannot be the heart of a hireling, motivated only by selfishness. But reward is not a selfish motive if you truly understand the biblical concept of rewards. Jesus unapologetically used the idea of reward as a motive for people to faithfully serve the Lord. The key is: do we understand what the reward is and what we will do with it?

Many Christians operate from an erroneous idea that the only thing that really matters about heaven is if you get to go there or not. In reality, we will not all hold an equal station in heaven. Some will go to heaven empty handed, while others will enter into eternity with reward that has accumulated from their days on earth. We don't want to simply squeak in the gate, but we ought to want to hear our Lord say, *"Well done, good and faithful servant, enter . . . into the joy of thy lord"* (Matthew 25:23). Today we want to look at the idea that our service will be rewarded.

📖 Read John 4:33–38. This is Jesus' response to the disciples when they interrupted His ministry to the woman at the well, and those she told about Him.

"But you shall receive power when the Holy Spirit has come upon you; and you shall be My witnesses both in Jerusalem, and in all Judea and Samaria, and even to the remotest part of the earth."

Acts 1:8

Producing Fruit   DAY FOUR

When the disciples tried to get Jesus to eat something, what did He say His food was?

_____

_____

_____

_____

What insights do you see from Christ's comparing Christian service to food?

_____

_____

_____

_____

What did Jesus say about the harvest (verse 35)?

_____

_____

_____

_____

What did He say about *"he who reaps"* (verse 36)?

_____

_____

_____

_____

In John 4, when Jesus encountered the woman at the well (an immoral Samaritan woman), His disciples were surprised that He took time to minister to her. When they tried to interrupt Him and get Him to eat, Jesus said to them, *"My food is to do the will of Him who sent Me and to accomplish His work"* (verse 34). It is an interesting comparison. If you think about it, Jesus is saying that to Him, spiritual work was like food. What is the purpose of food? It is necessary to sustain us, but it is also to satisfy us. In speaking of the harvest, Jesus says in verse 35, *"Lift up your eyes and look on the fields, that they are white for harvest."* In other words, "Don't wait; now is the time." The final statement (verse 36) is perhaps the most significant. He says, *"Already he who reaps is receiving wages and is gathering fruit for life eternal; so that he who sows and he who reaps may rejoice together."* There are wages for whatever roles we play in the spiritual harvest.

📖 Read 2 Corinthians 5:9–10.

What should the goal be for those who love the Lord (verse 9)?

_____

_____

_____

_____

What motive for serving Him do you see in verse 10?

_____

_____

_____

_____

The goal of every believer should be to please the Lord. But this passage goes on to speak of a very important motive for faithfully serving the Lord on earth. We will each appear before the "Judgment Seat of Christ." This is related to judging the works of a believer (1 Corinthians 3:10–15). In this judgment, it is not the person who is judged but the person's deeds, and not for salvation but for reward. The "Great White Throne" judgment (Revelation 20:11–15) differs in that, at that judgment which occurs at the end of time, all are judged (not just believers) regarding their eternal destiny based on whether or not their name is written in the "book of life." How will we be rewarded for the ministry we have on earth? The Bible speaks of spiritual reward in the form of "crowns" that we will receive in heaven.

The Bible identifies at least four crowns for different acts of faithfulness. Look at the passages below and identify the activity that results in reward in each of the passages.

James 1:12

_____

_____

_____

1 Corinthians 9:25

_____

_____

_____

2 Timothy 4:8

_____

_____

_____

1 Peter 5:4

_____

_____

_____

All believers will be rewarded for their faithfulness with crowns. The Bible identifies at least four crowns for different acts of faithfulness:

1) The "Crown of Life" (James 1:12; also mentioned in Revelation 2:10) is the reward for enduring trials.

2) The "Imperishable Crown" (1 Corinthians 9:25) is for running the race according to the rules.

3) The "Crown of Righteousness" (2 Timothy 4:8) is for loving His appearing.

4) The "Crown of Glory" (1 Peter 5:4) is for faithful church leaders. Some argue for a fifth crown, the "Crown of Exultation" (1 Thessalonians 2:19) for evangelism and discipleship, while others view this as being the same as the "Crown of Glory."

So we see that our service to the Lord will be rewarded. But what will become of these crowns we accumulate? Will we parade them around in heaven to boast of what we did for God? That would hardly be appropriate since the only acts that are rewarded are not what we do in our own strength, but what He does through us as we trust Him. Our righteousness is but *"filthy rags"* (Isaiah 64:6 KJV). Revelation 4:8–11 seems to suggest that the crowns will be used in heaven to worship Christ. In this passage we see the twenty-four elders laying their crowns down at the feet of Jesus. This puts the motive of reward into an entirely different perspective. I should want reward, not for selfish gain, but for the opportunity it affords to worship the One from whom all ministry flows. He alone is worthy of glory!

Doctrine
CROWNS

An easy way to remember the different crowns the Bible speaks of is the acrostic, **GIRL**.

G crown of glory

I imperishable crown

R crown of righteousness

L crown of life

Producing Fruit

DAY FIVE

FOR ME TO FOLLOW GOD

Jesus said, *"Follow Me, and I will make you fishers of men"* (Matthew 4:19). When we follow Him, He works changes in our lives. He changes our character, our values, and our priorities. As a result, He transforms us from selfish living that uses others for our own gain, into selfless living that seeks to be a blessing to others. In divine irony, God has so structured life that living for ourselves guarantees that our deepest needs go unmet, while living for others instead of self puts us in a place where the deep needs of our heart can be met. It is a lifestyle of faith. When we stop living only for self and trust God with our own needs, He not only meets them, but also uses us to meet them in others. God made each of us to be ministers. We are designed to be bearers of fruit, and we will be happy only when we are bearers.

Why Bother?

Why do I need to serve? Why can't someone else do it? What difference does it make if I serve or not? Is the little I have to offer going to make any real impact? First of all, we live in a needy world, and the non-Christian living only for self is not going to meet those needs. Second, the body of Christ (the Church) is *"fitted and held together . . . according to the proper working of each individual part."* The Church isn't what it is supposed to be without the contribution of every single member. (I have seen plenty of churches that aren't what they are supposed to be!) Third, apart from the needs of the world, apart from the needs of the church, I have a need. I was created for good works, and I will never be satisfied until I am doing them. Serving in kingdom ways, however small it may appear, makes a big difference in my enjoyment of life. If I live only for self, I may have pleasure for a season, but I will end up shallow and unfulfilled. If I serve, I find a significance that nothing else can come close to. It was Jesus who said, *"It is more blessed to give than to receive"* (Acts 20:35).

So where do you start? God must work in you if He is to be able to work through you.

So where do you start? God must work in you if He is able to work through you.

Consider your own growth in Christ. Jesus wants you to be a disciple—to abide in Him and allow His words to abide in you. He wants you to ask, and He wants to answer your prayers. He wants your life to glorify God. And He wants all of that to culminate in your life bearing much fruit.

APPLY As you look at your Christian life so far, what are some evidences you see of Christ making changes in your character?

_____

_____

_____

_____

_____

_____

Look at the list of the *"fruit of the Spirit"* from Galatians 5:22–23. Think about each area, and ask yourself, "Has God changed me in this area?"

Love

_____

_____

_____

_____

Joy

_____

_____

_____

Peace

_____

_____

_____

Patience

_____

_____

_____

_____

Kindness

_____

_____

"But the fruit of the Spirit is love, joy, peace, patience, kindness, goodness, faithfulness, gentleness, self-control; against such things there is no law."

Galatians 5:22–23

Goodness

_____

_____

_____

_____

Faithfulness

_____

_____

_____

_____

Gentleness

_____

_____

_____

_____

Self-Control

_____

_____

_____

_____

What are some evidences of His working through you for the benefit of others?

_____

_____

_____

What do you think your main spiritual gift might be?

_____

_____

_____

How can you develop that gift?

_____

_____

_____

Do not be discouraged if you long for more fruit than is yet evident. Fruit is not just the immediate results of your pursuit of God. It is also a gradual result of maturing. The longer you walk with the Lord, the more fruit you will bear. The key is to focus on the foundation, not the fruit.

Consider the five areas of John 15:7–8 and rate how you think you are doing.

ABIDING IN HIM
Not doing well   1   2   3   4   5   Doing well

HIS WORDS ABIDING IN YOU
Not doing well   1   2   3   4   5   Doing well

ASKING AND GETTING ANSWERS
Not doing well   1   2   3   4   5   Doing well

GLORIFYING GOD
Not doing well   1   2   3   4   5   Doing well

BEARING MUCH FRUIT
Not doing well   1   2   3   4   5   Doing well

The key to fruitfulness is not found in focusing on working more or working harder, but in walking more closely. It is not the job of the branch to produce fruit, but rather to bear it as a result of staying connected to the vine.

The main things that keep us in fellowship with God are: **1)** pursuing a relationship with Him through prayer and His Word, and **2)** dealing with sin as He reveals it by confessing and repenting.

As you close this week's lesson, write out a prayer to the Lord that reflects your heart on these two keys to abiding.

_____
_____
_____
_____
_____
_____
_____
_____
_____
_____
_____
_____
_____
_____
_____
_____
_____
_____
_____
_____

> *The key to fruitfulness is not found in focusing on working more or working harder, but in walking more closely.*

Notes

Part of a Whole

Imagine that you are cleaning your house when, under a couch cushion, you find one piece of a jigsaw puzzle. What would you do with it? What would it be worth? Probably several thoughts would go through your mind. First, you wouldn't be able to visualize the completed puzzle by looking at just one small piece. You might think about how frustrating it is to have one piece missing from a puzzle. Regardless, you will recognize that this piece serves little purpose apart from the rest of the puzzle. You might be asking, "What does this have to do with the subject of spiritual gifts?" I believe many people have a hard time figuring out their gifts and where they fit because they are focused on one piece of the proverbial puzzle instead of the complete picture. Such people try to define themselves as a whole instead of as a part of the whole. You see, every one of us is part of a whole that the Bible calls the "body of Christ." I really believe it is impossible to understand ourselves without understanding the body of Christ—the rest of the puzzle, if you will. God has designed each of us to be interconnected with each other. We each have a unique role in the kingdom, but we cannot define ourselves independently of each other. We are not the whole; we are part of the whole.

We are not the whole—we are part of the whole.

In John 1:18, we are told that no one has seen God at any time, but that Jesus, the only begotten son of God has *"explained"* Him. If you want to know what God is like, look at Jesus. In fact, one of His names, Immanuel, literally means "God with us." But the meaning of this name, Immanuel, presents a potentially confusing issue. God isn't "with" us at the present time in a visible, tangible sense. Forty days after Jesus was raised from the dead, He ascended into heaven. Before He ascended, He promised His followers that He wouldn't leave them as orphans and explained to them that the soon-to-come arrival of the Holy Spirit would be proof positive that God was still moving and working on earth. But how is God manifesting Himself in these last days? How is the Spirit of God moving on earth? The answers to these questions are found through answering another question. Where does the Holy Spirit dwell? He now resides in the hearts of believers. You see, the Holy Spirit is the Spirit of Christ (see Romans 8:9). When you became a Christian, the Holy Spirit took up residence in your heart. Therefore, Jesus is seen today in the lives of His followers. What He did individually during His earthly ministry He is doing through a corporate entity today—the Church. As Christians, we are the "body" of Christ; we are His hands, His feet, His heart. Because of this, the Christian cannot define himself apart from the Church, the worldwide body of Christ.

Part of a Whole   DAY ONE

THE STRUCTURE OF THE BODY

The human body really is amazing! Have you ever thought about how your body grows? God made it with the ability to take in nutrients, to process them, and then translate them into energy and mass. It is marvelously intricate. The body is even able to heal its own injuries, and in most cases is able to feed itself, care for itself, provide for itself, and even protect itself. God has given the human body everything it needs to become what He designed it to be. The human body doesn't need to borrow branches from a tree to have arms. It doesn't need the genes of an animal to become what it was meant to be. God put everything in the package; all you do is add water (and food of course).

There is a clear parallel between the human body and the body of Christ. Through God's empowerment, the Church is self-sustaining and self-contained. Money, man power, facilities, abilities—with Christ as the head, God has given the Church everything it needs to be what He wants it to be. Not believing in God's power has led many churches to adopt worldly methods for growth. But even if these methods do succeed in producing growth, it will not be God's growth. Psalm 127:1 says, *"Unless the Lord builds the house, they labor in vain who build it."* The secret of church growth isn't strategies; it is gifts.

📖 Look at 1 Corinthians 12:12–14.

What parallels does Paul mention between the human body and the body of Christ?

_____

_____

_____

What does it mean that we were all *"baptized into one body"* by one Spirit?

_____

_____

_____

_____

What do you think it means that we were all made *"to drink of one Spirit"*?

_____

_____

_____

_____

Word Study

BAPTISM

Our English word "baptism" is a translation of the Greek word *baptismos*. Culturally, one of the uses of the word was in the practice of dying cloth. A piece of cloth was "baptized" into a vat of dye, and thus took on the characteristics of the color of the dye. It would be forever identified with that new color. We are "baptized" or "identified" into the body of Christ.

In these verses, the apostle Paul uses the human body as a physical illustration of the body of Christ. He identifies a key element that links the two. He tells us that just like a human body, the body of Christ is one body, but has many different parts. As if for added emphasis, he repeats that idea in reverse, saying the many parts are still one body. In verse 13, he relates that we had our entry into that body by the ministry of the Holy Spirit. He uses the term *"baptized,"* which conveys the basic idea of identification—we were identified with Christ's body, the Church, by the Holy Spirit. He also says we all, being different (Jew or Greek, slave or free), drank of the same Spirit. The two are different, but related. The Spirit identifies us with the Church, but the Spirit in us helps the Church identify with us. His ministry in our lives produces unity with each other. Notice that Paul says we were **all** baptized, and **all** made to drink. This is not referring to some second work of grace that only some have partaken of, but to that which is true of all who are believers.

📖 Read 1 Corinthians 12:14–20.

In these verses Paul develops an analogy between the human body and the body of Christ. In Paul's analogy, what is the perceived problem with the foot and the ear (verses 15–16)?

_____

_____

_____

_____

How does Paul answer this problem in verses 17–20?

_____

_____

_____

_____

_____

_____

"But now God has placed the members, each one of them, in the body, just as He desired."

I Corinthians 12:18

In this analogy, Paul states that the problem with both the foot and the ear is one of perceived inferiority. Both are thinking that to be part of the body they have to be something other than what they are. In the same way, we are tempted to think the Church is really made up of preachers and singers while the rest of the people act as spectators. Notice he is not just saying they think themselves of no value. He is saying they think they aren't part of the body at all. In other words, they don't think they matter, and they have no responsibility within the Church. Paul's answer, using the need for hearing and smell, is that there are more needs in the human body than just sight. In the same way, the body of Christ needs more than just preaching and singing. One of the greatest weaknesses in many churches is that we define ministry too narrowly.

📖 Consider Paul's next problem in 1 Corinthians 12:21–25.

In Paul's example of the eye and the hand, what does Paul address as the problem (verse 21)?

_____

_____

_____

_____

How does Paul address this potential problem (verses 22–25)?

_____

_____

_____

_____

As Paul continues to develop this human body analogy, he makes an interesting point. He says an eye cannot say it doesn't need the hand, nor can a head say it doesn't need feet. Think about that. Two good eyes (or one good eye for that matter) can observe needs but can do absolutely nothing without assistance to make sure those needs are met. With only a head, a solution can be imagined, but it cannot be put into action. This potential danger for the Church as outlined in Paul's illustration is not the problem of inferiority, but of superiority. The eye and head don't recognize the value of others. Paul's solution is that Christians recognize that less important looking members are necessary and worthy (and in need) of more honor. We cannot allow feelings of inferiority or superiority to divide us in the body. We must all value each other, and that begins with valuing ourselves.

Paul goes on to say in verse 26, *"If one member suffers, all the members suffer with it."* Visualize yourself suffering a migraine headache. When your head is throbbing in pain, your feet are less effective. If one part is ill, the whole body feels it. That is the way it should be in the Church as well. Likewise, we ought to be able to rejoice with anyone who deserves honor.

📖 Paraphrase 1 Corinthians 1:27.

_____

_____

_____

_____

"Now you are Christ's body, and individually members of it."

1 Corinthians 12:27

You and I are part of Christ's body. He lives in us, and wants to be seen through us. We are the vessels through which He wants to work. We are all (corporately) the visible manifestation of Christ on the planet. And we are each one a part of it. None of us are the whole. We each are a part of the whole. It takes the participation of all of us for Jesus to be seen today.

A Body Is Supposed to Grow

A baby is born. If everything is normal, that baby will get hungry, and it will eat. Over time, it will grow. Not only will it grow in size, but it will grow in ability. How long will it grow? Hopefully, as long as it lives. Though it will stop growing in height at some point, it will not stop learning or developing. But it will reach a point called "maturity." There is a lot of talk today about how to have a growing church. One group tells you that the secret to a growing church is advertising. They suggest such strategies as television and radio spots or newspaper ads. Another group suggests that to grow you have to be the first to contact the new people in your area. There is even a service that will mail you names and addresses of everyone new who moves into your part of town. Another group believes that the key to a growing church is fitting in with the culture. People with this philosophy want you to focus less on teaching the Bible and talking about sin and more on addressing the heartfelt needs of the community by helping people "cope."

The advice of the experts goes on and on, yet sadly, most of these strategies focus on building a bigger church, not a better one. Most such strategies are based not on Scripture, but on secular business principles. The first century church had no such resources, and yet it experienced phenomenal growth— not just in numbers, but also in spiritual depth in the lives of its members. I am not saying that all church growth strategies are wrong, but they are only right if they follow scriptural strategies. What we are going to look at today is the major biblical passage on God's strategy for the growth of the Church.

You see, most modern church growth strategies concern themselves only with statistical growth, but God's goal for growth is different, and much more focused. As we look at what Scripture has to say, I think you'll see that strategies focusing on numbers put the cart before the horse, for biblically, spiritual growth must always precede statistical growth. Actually, statistical growth is the by-product; spiritual growth is the purpose of the body of Christ. This passage lists three goals God has for growth. Let's look at them.

📖 Read Ephesians 4:1–13 slowly so that you get the impact of the context.

Now, looking at verse 13, identify everything this verse says about God's goals for His church.

_____

_____

_____

_____

_____

In Ephesians 4:13, Paul lists three goals toward which every church should be ascribing: **a)** the unity of the faith and the knowledge of the Son of God, **b)** the attainment of a certain maturity level, and **c)** the measure of the stature which belongs to the fullness of Christ. What is the goal of church growth? It is that each of us reaches the finish line through accomplishing these three things.

📖 The "goals list" of verse 13 begins with *"the unity of the faith."* What do you think this means?

_____

_____

_____

_____

The body of Christ is made up of people from every nation, tribe, tongue, and people. We are very different, yet we are one body. Some believe that unity in the body of Christ means we must all believe exactly the same way. Others think it means we must all behave in exactly the same way. But those definitions are descriptions of unison, not unity. Two cats with their tails tied together have unison, but not unity. They both have a common belief (It isn't fun being tied to another cat!) and a common objective (to get free at all cost). They both work hard toward that objective, but one could hardly say that their actions are synonymous with unity. Imagine a symphony where every instrument kept hitting exactly the same note in exactly the same way. You could describe it in one word—BORING! No, a beautiful symphony is not music in unison, but music in unity—notes that blend together to make something they couldn't make separately. This is what God wants the body of Christ to be like, and, as we see in these verses, it all begins with relationship. What is it that unifies us? It is "the faith"—it is our common beliefs. The words "the faith" speak of the body of Christian doctrine and belief. One of the areas of which we are to be growing is the area of what we believe.

📖 The next phrase in Ephesians 4:13 is *"the knowledge of the Son of God."* How does this differ from the *"unity of the faith"*?

_____

_____

_____

How is it the same?

_____

_____

_____

We must grow in our doctrine, but it is possible to be doctrinally sound and spiritually dead. It is not enough to simply know about Christ. We must know Him. Of course, if we want to know Christ, we must seek to know all we can about Him. But it cannot stop there. We must pursue a relationship with Him. In the Greek construction, the knowledge of the Son of God really isn't a separate goal from *"the unity of the faith,"* but is part of it. The Greek word translated "knowledge" here is *epignosis*, which means "full, experiential, revealed knowledge." We are called to "know" Christ more

Word Study
FAITH

The Greek word translated faith in the Bible (*pistis*) is generally used in two different ways: to refer to our trust in God, or to refer to Christian doctrine—"the Faith." When doctrine is the meaning, usually the Greek word appears with the definite article (the Greek equivalent of our English word "the"). When trust is meant, usually the Greek word appears without the definite article. Here in Ephesians 4:13 "the faith" appears with that definite article.

and more. Twenty-five years after Paul became a Christian, he was still praying the following words: *"that I may know Him"* (Philippians 3:10).

📖 The next goal verse 13 reveals is *"to a mature man."* What do you think that means?

_____

_____

_____

_____

_____

_____

Paul says our goal is to become a "mature man." It should be acknowledged that this idea of maturity is not reserved for "a man" or men in general. The word "man" is generic here and should be taken to mean "person." The New International Version (NIV) captures this idea well, translating this part of verse 13 as *"until we all reach unity . . . and become mature."*

Let's look at this word "mature" or "perfect" as the King James Version translates it. In the Greek the word means, "full grown," "mature," "that which has accomplished its end, fulfilled its design." To be mature means we have fully realized our potential in the body of Christ. In other words, maturity is discovering what God designed for you individually and then fulfilling God's design corporately through the body of Christ's church.

The last goal verse 13 points us to is *"the measure of the stature which belongs to the fullness of Christ."* Reflect on that and write down your thoughts.

_____

_____

_____

_____

_____

_____

I would paraphrase this statement by saying "Christ is the measuring stick." How does a church reach full stature? Only if Christ is fully seen. When you add up all the parts—the individuals that make up the body—the whole should look like Jesus.

These goals may look like individual goals. Certainly each of us should be growing in our doctrine and in our relationship with Christ. Each of us is called to spiritual maturity. Each of us should be reflecting Christ in our lives. But perhaps the most important part of this verse is the word **"all."** It is not enough for you or me to arrive at maturity. We must help everyone else get there too!

Twenty-five years after Paul became a Christian he was still praying "that I may know Him" (Philippians 3:10).

HOW DOES THE BODY GROW?

Every Christian has a spiritual gift. Every believer is part of the church, the "body" of Christ. Sometimes we look at those with particular gifts and wish we were like them. But where would the body be if we all were the same? Where would the human body be with five noses and no ears? Where would it be with all hands and no feet? What good would it be to have three stomachs if you didn't have a heart? God has made the human body so that each part is needed. He has made the Church the same way. A body can function without ears or feet, but not as effectively. But some parts are so essential that there would be no life without them. Yet together, these parts make something they could never be separately. A heart is useless without blood vessels. A stomach is useless without a mouth. We all are needed in the body of Christ. What a wonderful thought! What value and significance this truth places on even the most unimportant looking parts!

📖 Read Ephesians 4:7–8 and summarize its message.

_____

_____

_____

_____

_____

_____

_____

Each and every one of us has received a special grace—a gift. It is part of our spiritual heritage. It is a result of Christ's victory. In Roman times, a conquering general would give gifts to the people from the spoils of war. Our conquering general has not only given us gifts, but the grace to exercise them.

📖 Look at Ephesians 4:11–12.

What spiritual gifts do you see here (verse 11)?

_____

_____

_____

_____

_____

What are these gifts to do (verse 12)?

_____

_____

_____

_____

_____

What is the result of these gifts being exercised (verse 12)?

_____

_____

_____

_____

Paul tells us here that God has given certain gifted individuals to the Church. Their role is not to do all the works of service, but to "equip" the saints so that they can serve. In other words, these gifted people (each of the roles is identified elsewhere as a leadership role) are to help each of us "saints" in the body be able to serve. We all have spiritual gifts. Ephesians 4:7 reminds us that *"to each one of us grace was given."* But these gifts need to be developed, and that is the purpose of the leaders in the church. As a result of their equipping ministry, we are able to serve, and the body of Christ (the Church) is built up. It becomes what God wants it to be.

📖 Take a look at Ephesians 4:15–16.

How is the body "fitted and held together"?

_____

_____

_____

_____

What causes the body to grow?

_____

_____

_____

_____

The Church is called the body of Christ. That body is both fitted and held together by that which every joint supplies. Maybe you don't consider yourself a joint, but the next part makes it obvious that this idea applies to you. It says that it is the *"proper working of each individual part"* that causes the growth and building up of the body. In other words, the body of Christ won't be all it is supposed to be apart from you. You are wanted and needed.

This idea of the church as the "body" of Christ is more than mere imagery. Think about the underlying message. When Jesus walked on earth, He was seen and heard—He made a difference. But what about today? He is in heaven now, so is He no longer seen and heard? Of course, He is seen and heard in us today! What Jesus was as an individual back then, the church is as an entity today. When each of us plays our part and serves as God has gifted us under the direction of Christ the head (verse 15), then Jesus is seen and recognized in the world today! When the parts of the body move, coordinated by the direction of the head, needs can be met; ministry can happen; lives can be changed—the world can be affected.

We are each parts of an incredibly significant whole. Our contribution is needed. Our input is valued and desired. We can aid in making Jesus seen

Today Jesus is seen and heard in us! What He was as an individual during His earthly ministry, the Church is as an entity today.

in a needy world. There is no room for feelings of insignificance on the part of any Christian. This is the point Jesus was making when He spoke of John the Baptist. He claimed that of those *"born of women"* there is no one greater than John. But He went on to say, *"Yet he who is least in the kingdom of God is greater than he"* (Luke 7:28). Jesus was showing the significance of those who are not only born of woman, but also born again of the Spirit of God. Though you may consider yourself the very least of these, Jesus says even the least is greater than John the Baptist!

Part of a Whole   DAY FOUR

THE RESULTS OF A GROWING BODY

Growing up with an older brother has its benefits as well as its challenges. I was grateful he was bigger than me when it came to the assignment of household chores. I'll never forget the time he tackled the neighborhood bully who was picking on me. But then again, sometimes, he picked on me. He could beat me in every sport. He would challenge me to arm wrestling and let me use both hands, and he still beat me. He always was allowed to do things that I was "too young to do." But I'll never forget the day during my junior year of high school when **I** challenged **him** to arm wrestling. After what seemed like an hour (but was more like two minutes) we were still deadlocked, and I was only using one arm! I didn't beat him that day, but he didn't beat me either. And you know, he has never arm-wrestled me since. I had grown up.

A mature body can do things that an immature body can't. Growing up has its privileges, but it also means greater responsibility. An adult body can do more—and it should! The body of Christ is supposed to grow, and I hope you appreciate now the fact that church growth is not simply a numbers game. The church is to grow in spiritual maturity. When it does, some wonderful things begin to happen. Today we will focus on some of the results of a maturing body.

📖 Take a look at Ephesians 4:14.

What does this verse say is the result of leaders equipping, laypeople serving, and all maturing?

_____

_____

_____

_____

_____

How do the goals of verse 13 guard us from the dangers mentioned in verse 14?

_____

_____

_____

_____

It is so important to see the progression of Ephesians 4. Jesus gives gifts to people (verses 7–8), and then He gives gifted people to the church (verse 11) for the purpose of equipping. The result is that saints begin doing the work of service, and the body is built up. Verse 13 identifies the goal of that building up, and in verse 14 we see a result of that "building up" process: maturity. We are no longer children. One of the marks of having matured in the ways verse 13 speaks of (the faith, knowing Christ, maturity, fully showing Christ) is that we are not carried away by *every wind of doctrine.* In other words, we don't fall prey to wrong thinking and wrong teaching, especially deceitful teachings. Why is doctrine so important? Because belief determines behavior. What we believe gives shape to how we live. It molds our choices. This is why Satan's greatest battleground is our minds.

What is our goal, according to Ephesians 4:15?

_____

_____

_____

We are called to *"grow up in all aspects"* until we reach Christlikeness. One fundamental we must recognize about ourselves is that none of us has arrived yet. In fact, though we may be very mature in some aspects, we may be infants in others. It doesn't do us much good to be mature in our doctrine if we are immature in our moral choices. Each of us has gaps in our spiritual growth, but being a part of a mature body, with all the gifts represented, will help each of us come to a place of balance in our growth.

Examine Ephesians 4:16 closely, taking a few minutes to think about each phrase and then answer the questions that follow.

How is the whole body fitted and held together?

_____

_____

_____

_____

What is the difference between being "fitted" and "held together"?

_____

_____

_____

What is a joint (think of it in terms of the human body)?

_____

_____

_____

What is caused by the *"proper working of each individual part"*?

_____

_____

_____

Extra Mile

CHRIST AS HEAD OF THE CHURCH

Christ is referred to as the "head" of the body (the Church) in each of these passages:

- 1 Corinthians 11:3
- Ephesians 1:22
- Ephesians 4:15
- Ephesians 5:23
- Colossians 1:18
- Colossians 2:10
- Colossians 2:19

With this imagery, Christ is understood as the intelligence of the Church, the source of direction, the guide of all the activities of the body, just as the brain is to the human body.

What will result if an individual part isn't working properly?

_____

_____

_____

_____

This one verse is filled with practical truth on what the body of Christ is supposed to be like. The body is both *"fitted and held together"* by that which every joint supplies. To be *"fitted"* may refer to an individual finding his or her proper place of service, and to be *"held together"* focuses on continuing to serve and function effectively in the area of giftedness. When you think of the term "joint" in this context, it would appear at a glance to be referring again to the individual, but in the human body a joint is that place where two bones meet. Applying that to the body of Christ, a "joint" may signify a relationship—that place where two parts of the body interact with each other. There is no ministry apart from relationships, and the stronger the relationships are, the more effective ministry becomes. It is an awesome thought to reflect on what the Church would be like if every individual part were working properly. I can't say that any church I have seen or been a part of does it perfectly. But the more effectively it happens, the more the church is able to build itself up. The body of Christ doesn't need to be more than what God intended it to be—it only needs to have every part properly working.

There is no ministry apart from relationships, and the stronger the relationships are, the more effective ministry becomes.

Part of a Whole **DAY FIVE**

FOR ME TO FOLLOW GOD

In our first lesson, we looked at the reality that each of us was created to have some kind of ministry. This week we have looked at the issue of ministry from the vantage point of the body as a whole. We must have some sense of the body of Christ if we are to ever discover our own place of ministry. We will not be able to define ourselves apart from each other, for no one of us is the whole. Consider the verses below and write their message in your own words.

Romans 12:6

_____

_____

_____

_____

_____

1 Corinthians 12:7

_____

_____

_____

_____

_____

Ephesians 4:7–8

_____
_____
_____
_____

1 Peter 4:10–11

_____
_____
_____
_____

The clear message of Scripture—the point made every time spiritual gifts are addressed—is that every believer has a spiritual gift. They aren't the same, but each of us has one. This fact guarantees that we are needed in the body of Christ. The Church is not all God wants it to be apart from our contribution. In addition, the fact that none of us has all the gifts guarantees that we need the ministry of others.

APPLY Have you ever doubted that you have a spiritual gift?

_____
_____
_____
_____

Christian pollster George Barna relates some startling statistics from recent surveys of Christians. From his Web site archives, I found these results from a 1995 survey:

Seventy-one percent of churchgoers say they have heard of spiritual gifts. But only twenty-two percent can identify a spiritual gift they possess. Twelve percent claim they do not have a spiritual gift.

More startling than these statistics was the fact that among those who identify a spiritual gift they possess, roughly a third (31%) listed characteristics or qualities which are not identified as spiritual gifts in the Bible. They mentioned such things as love, kindness, relationships, singing, and listening. What this tells me is that the Church has not done a very good job of teaching what the Bible says about spiritual gifts. No wonder so many believers are not actively involved in serving.

In addition to scores of people not serving in their churches, another problem lies in the fact that many who are serving are finding their service frustrating and ineffective. Many are burned out. There are several reasons for this. One is that too few are doing the work of service. Another reason is that people are being asked to do things they are not equipped to do. A third significant reason is that often people are serving outside of their giftedness. As a result, they are drained by their service, and they see few results. But it may be that the problem is simply that they haven't yet found where they fit. Let me illustrate what I mean. A hammer is designed to hammer nails. When I

Did You Know?
SPIRITUAL IGNORANCE

According to a recent survey by the George Barna Research organization, only about 22% of churchgoers can identify a spiritual gift they possess, and about one third of that number identified something other than those things Scripture identifies as spiritual gifts.

use it for that purpose, it is perfect; it has realized its purpose. Pliers are not designed for hammering nails; have you ever tried to hammer a nail with a pair of pliers? They can do it, but not nearly as well as a hammer. Both are great to have in your toolbox, and neither is more valuable to the carpenter than the other. Christian maturity means learning your giftedness, finding where you fit in the body, and then living out your giftedness. The problem in most churches and ministries is that there are a lot of pliers hammering nails. Do you think you have matured in the sense of understanding your own giftedness and finding where that fits in the work of God?

We saw in 1 Corinthians two potential problems in body life. One is the problem of people who don't see their own worth. They have feelings of inferiority, and they doubt that their gift really matters.

 Have you ever struggled with such feelings?

_____

_____

_____

_____

What does today's lesson say to you about this?

_____

_____

_____

_____

SPIRITUAL DANGERS

There are two dangers of wrong thinking about spiritual gifts:

✓ Inferiority (My gift doesn't matter.)

✓ Superiority (Your gift doesn't matter.)

Faith is being willing to take God at His Word. We must trust God when He says we have a gift, and we must trust the gift He in His wisdom chose to give us.

Another potential problem in body life is not seeing the worth of others. Every spiritual gift suffers from the potential danger of tunnel vision. Having a gift, we will automatically be passionate about that type of ministry. If we aren't careful, we may move from thinking that kind of ministry really matters to thinking it is the only kind that matters. We may develop feelings of superiority, as if we are doing the really important work.

 Do you ever struggle with undervaluing the service of others?

_____

_____

_____

_____

What do you need to do differently?

_____

_____

_____

_____

Why not write out a prayer to close this week's lesson. In it, be sure to thank God for how He has gifted you, as well as for how He has gifted others. Pray for your church, that everyone would find where he or she fits, so the church can be built up by the proper working of each individual part.

_____
_____
_____
_____
_____
_____
_____
_____
_____
_____
_____
_____
_____
_____
_____
_____
_____
_____
_____
_____
_____

Notes

Understanding Spiritual Gifts

(1 CORINTHIANS 12:1–12)

No nation draws together more than when it is at war. This was certainly true of the United States during World War II. Certainly, America could not have succeeded in defeating her enemies without well-trained and courageous soldiers in large numbers. These were the paid professionals of war. But the soldiers could not win the war alone. They needed the backing of the entire nation. Everyone was a part of the action; kids collected scrap metal and rubber; women filled the factory jobs the soldiers left behind; elderly ladies rolled bandages; retired men helped fill the work force; families invested in government bonds; and entire businesses were retooled to produce the weapons of war.

An infantry soldier needs to be an accurate marksman. But the best shot in the world is no good without a working weapon and adequate ammunition. What good is a skilled pilot without an airplane? During World War II, all of these weapons of war were made back home by a nation of families who all had a sense of ownership in the war strategy. Even if they didn't have a son "over there," they probably had a friend or neighbor who did. In the evenings, whole families circled around the radio to listen to President Roosevelt's "fireside chats" and the latest war updates. Everyone contributed in differing ways, as they were able, toward the common purpose of winning the war.

Everyone's role is important!

This war example is a picture of what the church is supposed to be like. We're not at peace; we're at war with the enemies of God, and we can't live "business as usual" lives. This battle, like every other, won't be won only by the soldiers, but by the nation. In 1 Samuel 30:24, David instituted a statute for Israel, stating that when the war was over, the share of the spoils for one who stayed with the baggage would be the same as for one who went into battle. His point was that everyone's role is important, not just those on the front lines. This is true of gifts as well. Every gift is needed, and I believe this passage shows the heart of God: in heaven, the believer who is faithful with his or her gift of service or mercy will be rewarded in equal measure to the faithful teacher or leader. All are important to God's work.

DAY ONE

A CHURCH IN NEED OF INSTRUCTION

One of the ways God has insured that all have a part in His work is through His giving each and every one of us a spiritual gift. Through His Spirit living in us, God has enabled each of us to have something to offer. He has empowered each of us to be a blessing and a benefit to others. A spiritual gift is a supernatural, spiritual endowment. A spiritual gift is not simply a learned ability. Everyone can learn how to teach more effectively; in fact, to be an elder in a church (aside from other scriptural requirements), one has to be able to teach. But this doesn't mean everyone has to have the gift of teaching. Effectiveness requires the energizing work of the Spirit. Today we will begin looking at one of the main passages on the subject of spiritual gifts. To fully appreciate it though, we need to understand a bit of the context of the book in which it appears. If you'll be patient, I promise your effort will be rewarded.

📖 Look up 1 Corinthians 1:4–7 and record what you learn there about gifts in the Corinthian church.

_____

_____

_____

_____

The church at Corinth was a blessed church. When Paul speaks of the *"grace"* of God which was given to them in Christ, it is helpful to remember that the Greek word translated *"spiritual gifts"* literally means "the results of grace." Paul reminds them they had been enriched in everything related to speech and knowledge (verse 5). Most significantly, Paul reminds them that as a church they were *"not lacking in any gift."* You would think this would be a pretty healthy church, but as we will soon see, it was not.

📖 Consider Paul's words in 1 Corinthians 1:10–11 in the light of verses 4–7 and write your observations.

_____

_____

_____

As amazing as it may seem, here was a church with all the gifts, yet instead of the members being a blessing to each other, their church was dominated by divisions and quarrels. We see this problem reiterated in 1 Corinthians 12:25, where Paul writes, *". . . that there should be no division in the body. . . ."* In 1 Corinthians 1:29 Paul instructs, *". . . that no man should boast before God,"* and again in verse 31, *"'LET HIM WHO BOASTS, BOAST IN THE LORD.'"* It would seem that this was a church where people were more interested in showboating than in serving. They wanted to exercise their gifts, but they weren't doing it God's way. Unfortunately, that temptation did not die out in the first century.

There is no small irony in the fact that the letter where Paul spends the most time discussing spiritual gifts is to a church that lacked no gifts. Throughout the entire epistle of 1 Corinthians, Paul confronts one problem after another in this fleshly church. Clearly, Paul felt they were in great need of instruction on the subject of gifts. He spends chapters 12 and 14 teaching them details about the proper (and improper) functioning of gifts, and sandwiches in between those chapters a discourse on love. Don't miss the obvious point here: if our gifts don't benefit our relationships, then we aren't using them correctly.

📖 Read 1 Corinthians 12:1–12 carefully and reflectively. What main points stand out to you?

_____

_____

_____

_____

As we look at 1 Corinthians 12, we must understand the context. Here Paul isn't emphasizing the gifts themselves; in fact, he only spends four verses on them. Paul wants the Corinthians to appreciate the many different gifts there are, but more importantly, he wants to teach them the proper ways to use the gifts. He begins this chapter by exhorting them, *"I do not want you to be unaware."* He wanted them to have a proper understanding of spiritual gifts.

📖 Now look at 1 Corinthians 12:4–6.

What words are repeated in each of these three verses?

_____

_____

_____

What ideas are repeated?

_____

_____

_____

The main words that we find repeated in each of these three verses are the words "varieties" and "same." What Paul emphasizes here is the nature of the gifts. His two main points are the diversity of the gifts and the unity of the gifts. Also note the repeated idea of God as the source of gifts. In verse 4, Paul speaks of differing gifts, *"but the same Spirit."* In verse 5, the term is *"the same*

Each member of the Trinity has a role in the exercise of our spiritual gifts.

Lord." In verse 6, it is *"the same God"* who works the effect of each person's gift. Notice the progression here. It is the Spirit who gives us our gift. It is the Lord who gives us our ministry. (In the New Testament, the term "Lord" is used almost exclusively of Christ.) It is God the Father, who brings the results to our service. Each member of the Trinity has a role in the exercise of our spiritual gifts. All that God is comes into play to enable us to serve Him.

Our giftedness comes from the Holy Spirit. Our ministry comes from the Lord Jesus. Our results come from God the Father.

THE ORIGIN OF OUR OPPORTUNITIES

Every believer receives a gift, even carnal believers, as 1 Corinthians illustrates. But as chapter 12 shows, everyone doesn't get the same gift. Think what a boring world it would be if everyone was the same or had the same abilities. Think of how incomplete the body would be if everyone had the same gift. A second reality is that no one gets all the gifts. If we had all the gifts, we wouldn't need each other. But God didn't design it that way. You see, everyone lacks something. This insures we need the gifts of others. The most important thing isn't what your gift is, but where you got it. It is from God. The Holy Spirit doesn't give anything that isn't supernatural, valuable, and good. James 1:17 tells us God only gives good gifts—it's part of His unchanging nature. Therefore, dissatisfaction with our gift indicates a mistrust of God. If we are jealous or envious of someone else's gift, it shows we don't trust God or believe His way is best. Romans 12:2 says God's will is always *"good and acceptable and perfect."* That is true of the gift He gave you. Your giftedness is God's choice, not yours.

📖 Compare 1 Corinthians 12:4 with 12:11 and write down what you learn there about the source of your gifts and the reason you have the gifts you have.

_____

_____

_____

_____

Verse 4 tells us there are different gifts, but they all come from the same Spirit. If you are a Christian, you can be sure the Holy Spirit has given you some kind of endowment for the good of the body. In verse 11, Paul repeats himself, as if for emphasis. He instructs us that all the different gifts come from the same source—the Spirit of God. Furthermore, Paul tells us that our gift was distributed to us *"just as He wills."* Our gift—whatever it is—was picked for us by God.

📖 We saw in verse 4 that there are *"varieties of gifts,"* and we see here in verse 5 that there are *"varieties of ministries."* What do you think is the difference between the two?

_____

_____

_____

_____

Word Study
WILL

1 Corinthians 12:11 tells us the Spirit distributes our gift *"just as He wills."* The Greek word translated "will" here is not the usual word translated God's will (*thelema*), which is to be followed, but rather is *boulema*, which has a different emphasis. *Thelema* emphasizes God's will as a direction to follow. *Boulema* emphasizes God's will from the standpoint of the counsel preceding the decision. In other words, it is not just that God wants us to have a particular gift, but He emphasizes the forethought involved in giving us that particular gift.

How you are able to exercise your gift is just as sovereignly bestowed as the gift itself. Our opportunities to serve come from God as well. If you want to find where you fit, don't jump ahead of God and run around trying to create opportunities for yourself. That is the world's way. True ministry is received, not achieved. In Acts 20:24, the apostle Paul said, *"But I do not consider my life of any account as dear to myself, so that I may finish my course and the ministry which I* **received** *from the Lord Jesus, to testify solemnly of the gospel of the grace of God."* In Colossians 4:17, Paul wrote, *"Say to Archippus, 'Take heed to the ministry which you have* **received** *in the Lord, that you may fulfill it'"* [emphasis added in both verses]. Our giftedness is as the Spirit wills, not as we will. Likewise, our ministry is received from the Lord according to His plan, not achieved by us according to ours.

Another way of stating the message of verse 5 is that there are different **opportunities**, but the same **Lord** gives them. The same gift isn't always exercised in the same way. If God gave you the gift of teaching, He may let you exercise it in front of thousands of people, or He may want you to use it to teach twelve third graders. It is His choice, not yours. In fact, if you're not faithful with those third graders, why would God trust you to teach thousands?

📖 Look at Psalm 78:71.

What was David doing when God called him to be king?

_____

_____

How was his new role similar to his previous one?

_____

_____

_____

_____

Psalms 78:71 tells us God took David from the care of sheep to be the shepherd of Israel. David had already proven himself a faithful shepherd, so God gave him a bigger flock. Does this mean if we are faithful in a small job God will give us the biggest job? Not necessarily, but clearly opportunities to serve may be lost because of unfaithfulness.

Understanding that my ministry is received from the Lord eliminates competition. Competition in the Church is a most grievous sin. Unfortunately, I see it all too often among pastors. It is sad, but at my denomination's annual convention, the most frequent questions aren't "How is your walk with God?" or "What are you learning?" but "How big are your services?" or "How big is your budget?" It is all too easy to try to measure our worth by comparing ourselves to each other instead of by whether or not we are being faithful. The example of the widow and the two mites she gave at the Temple graphically illustrates that God is not simply concerned with who does the most, but rather with what we do with what we have. Understanding these principles also negates pride. Instead of boasting, we must say, "I am filling a role God gave me, not one I earned."

True ministry is received, not achieved.

"From the care of the ewes with suckling lambs He brought him, to shepherd Jacob His people, And Israel His inheritance."

Psalms 78:71

DIFFERING RESULTS

John Wesley is one of the fathers of the church in America. His ministry has spanned centuries, with the results long outlasting his life. Yet, if you read his journals, you discover an interesting fact. He was never one to try to measure his effectiveness. The oft-repeated refrain in his writings is "preached at such and such a place—many seemed deeply moved, but God alone knows how deeply." Sadly, today everything seems to be about numbers. We are constantly trying to measure ourselves, as if we must justify our existence. But can we ever measure accurately? What if we saw hundreds saved? Are we then more important than the person or ministry who only saw one convert? Modern logic would say "yes," but in reality, such questions can only be answered by God in eternity. D. L. Moody preached the gospel to some two hundred million people in his lifetime—all without the aid of television. Yet who had the greater impact, D. L. Moody or the man who came to his shoe store one day and explained to him the plan of salvation?

📖 1 Corinthians 12:6 tells us that the working out of our gifts will have different *"effects."* What do you think this means?

_____

_____

_____

_____

Someone once said, "You can count the number of seeds in an apple, but you cannot count the number of apples in a seed." Verse 6 tells us there are *"varieties of effects."* In other words, the same service, with the same Spirit working, does not always produce the same results. That's okay. Think about a water faucet. What is more important, how much water it pours out, or that it pours out as much as the master desires? What really matters is that God's purpose is accomplished.

According to verse 6, who is the author of the effect of your service, and what does that mean to you?

_____

_____

_____

_____

Verse 6 makes it clear that there are differing results, but one God who *"works all things in all persons."* He is the source of results, not us. There is nothing at all wrong with results, nothing wrong with the spectacular, but it is wrong to place our focus there. Jesus was never impressed with His own miracles. Talking to the woman at the well was just as important to Him as feeding the five thousand. We won't know for sure until we are in heaven, but Scripture indicates that the woman at the well was instrumental in leading many to Christ. We see no such record for the five thousand. The important thing isn't the results we see, for we will never fully see the results of our faithfulness this side of heaven. The important thing is that Christ is the source of our service. If Christ is the source, then the effect is God's design no matter how big or small. Our preoccupation with results, with statistics, with "bigger and better," is of the flesh and reflects worldly values.

📖 Read 1 Corinthians 3:10–15 and jot down what it says (or doesn't say) about the size of our service.

_____

_____

_____

_____

_____

_____

When the day arrives for our works to be judged, the important thing will not be the quantity of works, but their quality. The contrast in 1 Corinthians 3 is between the person who walks in the Spirit and the one who walks after the flesh. When our works are judged, what we did in our own strength will be *"wood, hay,* [and] *straw"* and it will not last. But what God did through us, is *"gold, silver,* [and] *precious stones."* It not only survives the fire of judgment, but is purified by it.

The effect of our service is the wrong place to put our focus. Focusing on effects brings **false pride** or a false sense of **failure**. Let me illustrate this for you. Let's say an evangelist is instrumental in one hundred souls being saved. "Praise the Lord!" we shout. A sick member is healed, and we excitedly say things like, "It's a miracle!" or "Thank you Jesus!" Someone with the gift of service signs up to work in the nursery. Nobody yells, "Man, what a nursery worker! Did you see the way she changed that diaper?" It takes just as much a work of the Spirit for a person with the gift of service to serve as it does for an evangelist to give an altar call. And a distracted mom, taking care of her baby because there was no nursery, probably isn't going to be coming down to the altar at the end of the service.

In addition, focusing on effects deifies the **servant** instead of the **Savior**. The nursery worker who is faithful and Spirit-filled will be just as rewarded in heaven as the faithful pastor or evangelist. Both gifts (service and teaching) must be exercised in God's power. Understanding this eliminates pride, bragging, and hero-worship. Our reward is not based on the **effect** of our service, but on the **source** of it.

We saw in Ephesians 4 that God is concerned about the unity of the body. One of the things that this passage makes clear is that church unity doesn't depend on the **service** but on the **source**.

Unity depends on the Spirit of God being in control of each of us and manifesting Himself as He wills. All don't have the same **gift**. But, unity doesn't depend on our giftedness. All don't **serve** the same way. Unity doesn't depend on our service either. All don't have the same **effect,** but unity doesn't depend on this either. Unity is the automatic result if God is the source of our service, because He is always one with Himself.

Importance should not be placed upon visible results, but upon the idea that Christ is the source of our service.

✏ *Did You Know?*
(?) **BESTOW HONOR**

1 Corinthians 12:23 tells us, " . . . those members of the body, which we deem less honorable, on these we bestow more abundant honor." Though pastors, missionaries, evangelists, and other high-profile ministers should be applauded for their service, how refreshing it would be to applaud those who are not usually in the spotlight, such as ushers and nursery workers.

FOR THE COMMON GOOD

W hile we read Paul's words to the Corinthian church, we must continually bear in mind his assessment of that church. They were not the model of spiritual health. His teaching is designed to correct problems that existed in their understanding of gifts, and therefore, in their use of them. They had a lot of growing to do. In 1 Corinthians 3 he calls them *"babes in Christ."* He rebukes them, saying, *". . . since there is jealousy and strife among you, are you not fleshly, and are you not walking like mere men?"* In other words, Paul says that their lives were no different than the lives of unbelievers. Instead of serving one another, they were shoving each other aside in attempts to take center stage. They didn't understand the main purpose of spiritual gifts.

📖 Hopefully, by now you have come to the biblical conclusion that every Christian has at least one spiritual gift. Look at 1 Corinthians 12:7 and see how this verse supports this idea.

_____

_____

_____

Each Christian has a *"manifestation of the Spirit."* God, who lives in the heart of every believer, expresses Himself in a unique way through each believer. You have an endowment by virtue of being a Christian. The gift or gifts endowed to you will differ from what has been endowed to other Christians, but you can rest assured that the moment you trusted Christ and the Holy Spirit came into your life, you were endowed with at least one spiritual gift.

📖 As you read verse 7, identify the overarching purpose of every spiritual gift and write down your thoughts on that.

_____

_____

_____

_____

This is perhaps the most important point of our entire lesson today. Be sure you don't miss this. Spiritual gifts are for *"the common good."* The reason God gave you a gift was so you could give a blessing to the body. Your gift is not for your own personal edification. It is for someone else. Therefore, when we do not exercise our gifts in serving, we rob others of something God wants to give them through us. Certainly, we are edified when we serve others, but that is not the purpose of our gift—it is a by-product.

Understanding the truths of verse 7 will eliminate jealousy, envy, and pride (all problems at Corinth). God has placed you in a specific church and ministry because He needs you there to accomplish what He wants done through that church and ministry. God has provided each of us an opportunity to serve, and we will not be satisfied unless we are finding it and fulfilling it.

Spiritual gifts are "for the common good" (1 Corinthians 12:7). Think of what an incredible church your church would be if everyone acted in order to benefit others.

📖 Read the list of gifts in 1 Corinthians 12:8–10.

What gifts are absent from this list that you would expect to be there?

_____

_____

Why do you think those aren't included?

_____

_____

_____

Verses 8–10 are the most lengthy attempt 1 Corinthians makes at a list of different gifts. It is important to recognize that the goal of this passage is not to give an exhaustive list, but rather to emphasize the concept of unity in diversity. Some of the most significant gifts are conspicuously absent. This list makes no mention of the equipping gifts of teaching or exhortation. There is also no reference to the gift of leading or mercy.

As you look at verses 8–10, one important fact will escape your notice if you are not studying it in the Greek. You will notice in your English text that the word "another" is repeated frequently in these verses. What your English text will not show you is that there are two different Greek words for "another" with decidedly different meanings, both of which are used in these verses. The first time "another" appears, it is translated from the Greek word *állos*, which means "another of the same kind." It is from this word that our English term "ally" is derived. The next time the word "another" appears in our text (verse 9), it is from the Greek word *heteros*, which means "another of a different kind."

What Paul has done in the Greek, which is not apparent in the English, is he has grouped these gifts into categories. Each time he uses the term *héteros,* he is introducing a new category or grouping of gifts. All within each category share common similarities, but each grouping is separate and distinct from the others. Now, what this tells us is that Paul is not trying to give us a complete list of all the gifts, but to show us two important truths: **a)** there are different categories of gifts, and **b)** there are various similar gifts within each category. Your assignment is to identify each category and give it a name. To help you, I will show you each occurrence of the word *héteros*, so you will be able to find the transitions to new categories. The first transition marked by the use of the word *héteros* instead of *állos* is the first "another" in verse 9, and the second transition is the "another" before *"various kinds of tongues"* in verse 10. Once you have identified your categories, name them and list all the different gifts within them.

_____

_____

_____

_____

_____

_____

Paul's first category of gifts is found in verse 8. He groups together the *"word of wisdom"* and the *"word of knowledge."* This would seem to be a category of intellectual gifts. The second group includes faith, gifts of healing, effecting of miracles, prophecy, and distinguishing of spirits. This group would seem to be supernatural (and perhaps situational) endowments. The third grouping of gifts includes various kinds of tongues and interpretation of tongues. This would be the language group of gifts. We will talk more later about differing views in the body of Christ on exactly how these gifts function, but for now, keep your focus on the main thing Paul is saying. There are different categories of gifts given by the will of the Spirit for the common benefit of the body. These aren't the only gifts, but they are examples of the point Paul makes.

What is your gift(s)? I can't say. But I can tell you this much about your giftedness: it isn't for you. God gave you what He wanted you to have so you would be a benefit and a blessing to others. He wants to manifest Himself through you. Think of what an incredible church your church would be if everyone acted in order to benefit others.

FOR ME TO FOLLOW GOD

The body of Christ was God's idea. The earthly ministry of Jesus did not end when He ascended. For ten days after the ascension (until Pentecost), the followers of Jesus waited and prayed. But on Pentecost, something new was born. The Spirit of God took up residence in the people of God, so God could still be seen. This new entity, called the Church, would be the way God would manifest Himself to the unbelieving world. Who Jesus was as an individual—teaching, encouraging, confronting, and manifesting the power of God—the Church now is as an entity. We stretch across the globe, and through us, Jesus manifests Himself every day in a myriad of ways. He doesn't manifest all of God through any one individual. There is great diversity in how He has gifted each person in the body. He manifests some of God through each of us so that through all of us God can be seen and glorified. The net result of all of the parts put together is one picture—God. It's about Him, not us. If ever our gifts become about us instead of Him, they cease to fulfill their purpose.

 We saw in Day One that each member of the Trinity plays an important and unique role in our service. The Spirit gives us our gift, but it is from the Lord Jesus that we receive our ministry, and it is God the Father who produces the effect of our service. Where are you in that process?

At this point, what do you believe to be your giftedness from the Spirit?

_____

_____

_____

_____

_____

Do you have a sense of having received a particular ministry from the Lord Jesus?

_____

_____

_____

_____

Is this sense reinforced by opportunities to serve in that way?

_____

_____

_____

Do you see God-given results to your service?

_____

_____

_____

_____

Are you able to trust God with the size and scope of those results?

_____

_____

_____

_____

"Receiving" a ministry may begin with a sense of calling to a particular type of service, but we cannot truly say we have "received" a ministry until the Lord opens that particular door. Desire must be met with opportunity.

It is important to evaluate where you are right now, for it is from these evaluations that the Lord will direct your applications of what you are learning. You don't have to know all the answers yet, but it will be helpful if you seek the Lord about the next step in the process.

We saw from the example of David in Psalm 78:71 that God took him from caring for sheep and gave him Israel as a flock. David, who had been faithful with the small flock, was given a larger one. In the parable of the talents (Matthew 25:14–30), Jesus told a story of a master who gave money to three servants to invest while he was away. When he returned, he blessed those who had been faithful stewards of what he entrusted to them. For the one who had been unfaithful with his talent, however, there was wrath.

Look at Matthew 25:28. What did the master do with the talent He had entrusted to the faithless servant?

_____

_____

_____

That man's talent was taken away and given to another who had been faithful. There is a lesson in this for us as we consider spiritual gifts and opportunities to serve.

As you reflect on this, jot down any areas of service God brings to mind where you need to be more faithfu.l Then talk with God about this area.

_____

_____

_____

_____

There is a danger for each of us in misinterpreting the results of our service.

We saw in 1 Corinthians 12:6 that there are *"varieties of effects"* of our service. There is a danger for each of us in misinterpreting the results of our service. We saw that, in abundance of results, there can be a false sense of pride, and with few visible results, there can be a false sense of failure. Consider each of these scenarios and write down some examples you have seen in your own life.

FALSE PRIDE	FALSE SENSE OF FAILURE
_____	_____
_____	_____
_____	_____
_____	_____
_____	_____
_____	_____
_____	_____
_____	_____

Close out this week's lesson by writing a prayer to the Lord expressing what you have learned.

_____

_____

_____

_____

_____

_____

_____

_____

_____

_____

_____

_____

_____

_____

Notes

Understanding the Types of Spiritual Gifts

Much confusion surrounds the subject of spiritual gifts in the body of Christ today. At times, it seems the only thing we can all agree on is that we don't agree at all. Often, differing views on gifts and their functions produce great schisms among believers that make unity in the body of Christ quite difficult. One group believes that some gifts are no longer functioning. Others believe that if you don't demonstrate or display certain gifts, you aren't filled with the Spirit. Some aren't sure what the difference is between spiritual gifts and natural talents, while others aren't convinced that everyone has gifts. One group accuses others of excess, while another accuses some of neglect. Pride abounds on every side of the argument, as does judgment and criticism. Each side can point to passages of Scripture to support its conclusions. Sometimes, divergent groups point to the same passage to defend their convictions, and much disagreement exists on the correct way to interpret those passages. How did we get here? Is this what the Lord had in mind when His Spirit came at Pentecost?

One can only wonder what the Lord thinks of the state of things today. He must surely be grieved. But there is a solution. There must be. In fact, faith requires that we look for such a solution, and we will find it in only one location: the Scriptures. *"Now*

"Now concerning spiritual gifts, brethren, I do not want you to be unaware."

—Luke 6:44

concerning spiritual gifts," the apostle Paul writes, *"I do not want you to be unaware"* (1 Corinthians 12:1). There are two problems that have produced the present state of confusion and division. First, a great many Christians are simply uninformed of what the Bible teaches about spiritual gifts. Second, among those who have studied spiritual gifts, many (if not most) have camped on a favorite passage that agrees with and supports their own experience and bias to the neglect of other passages. Few Christians have taken the time to try to weave each of the four major passages together. But that is what we must do if we are to ever have God's mind on the subject, *"for God is not a God of confusion but of peace"* (1 Corinthians 14:33).

Ample evidence exists to back up the claim that God is not an author of confusion. For starters, there is only one God, not many different Gods working in different ways. There is one faith, not several. There is one body and one Spirit. Ephesians 4:6 tells us there is *"one God and Father of all who is over all and through all and in all."* For this very reason, unity in the body of Christ is not only possible, it is to be expected. In Ephesians 4:3, Paul admonishes us to be *"diligent to preserve the unity of the Spirit in the bond of peace."* Notice, he does not charge us to produce unity, but to preserve it. We cannot produce unity—only God can do that. But unity is *"of the Spirit,"* and when He rules in your heart and mine, unity is automatic. It is preserved as we guard His rule and reign in our lives.

Understanding the Types   DAY ONE

SEEING THE SUBJECT FROM ALL SIDES

Perhaps the best way to understand how we can all look at the subject of spiritual gifts and draw such differing conclusions is that we are not all looking from the same vantage point. There are four passages in the New Testament that address the subject of spiritual gifts. We will look at these passages in the following order: Ephesians 4:11–12; 1 Peter 4:10–11; 1 Corinthians 12; and Romans 12:1–16. Each of these four passages offers us a limited view of the topic, but none gives the whole picture. They do not give us a glimpse of different interpretations, but act as separate windows, all looking into the same room from divergent angles. Each window or passage reveals a different perspective on the spiritual gifts issue. To grasp the whole, we must gain a balanced view of each of the parts. Today, we are going to piece together the biblical mosaic on spiritual gifts and attempt to bring the big picture into focus.

The four passages do not present four different doctrines; however they do present us with four different vantage points from which we can view the same truth. When you juxtapose these passages, you find three main categories of gifts:

equipping gifts (sometimes called "speaking" gifts because they all involve speaking the Word of God)

edifying gifts (also called "serving" gifts)

evidence gifts (also called "sign" gifts because they serve to bear witness to the truth and power of God)

Although many studies attempt to come up with an all-encompassing list of the gifts mentioned in Scripture, this will not be our purpose in this study. Instead, we will focus on the main point of each of the lists and move from there. In

Scripture, the plain things are often the main things. The passage we will focus on today is Ephesians 4. As you examine each of the four major texts, your key focus should be to identify the main objective of the text's author (Paul or Peter). Keep in mind that we won't examine every single detail of these passages in this lesson. What we want to focus on is "the big picture" of spiritual gifts.

📖 Take a few minutes to review Ephesians 4:11–12.

Which of the three main categories of gifts are represented here?

_____

_____

_____

Place all the gifts mentioned in this passage into the categories they most closely fit:

equipping gifts

_____

_____

edifying gifts

_____

_____

evidence gifts

_____

_____

_____

Here in Ephesians 4, the main focus is on only one of the three categories: equipping gifts. There is no mention here of evidence gifts. In verse eleven we find five gifts directly identified as functioning in the process of equipping the saints: apostleship, prophecy, evangelism, pastoring and teaching (although you can see how some draw the conclusion that pastor and teacher are linked as one instead of separate). Verse 12 instructs us that these four or five serve the purpose of "equipping the saints for the work of service." In other words, their main job is to help others do an effective job of serving. While certainly they can and should "edify" others, equipping is their job description. The edifying (or serving) gifts are not as noticeable in this particular text, but they would be implied as part of "the work of service" that saints are equipped to do.

📖 As you look at Ephesians 4:11 in its context, what do you think is Paul's main point?

_____

_____

_____

Paul's main point is that the gifts mentioned in verse 11 exist for equipping the saints so the body can be built up through their serving. This idea of the body being built up is mentioned in verse 12 and again in verse 16. When leaders equip and everyone serves, the body is "edified" or built up. This obviously refers to more than just numeric growth, since, as we saw in an earlier lesson regarding verse 13, the goal is maturity.

Paul lists five specific "equipping" roles here. But are they really gifts? If not, what are they?

_____

_____

_____

_____

_____

The questions in this exercise are hardly simple questions that deserve simple answers. While we see prophecy and teaching listed elsewhere as spiritual gifts, the wording here emphasizes the person more than the task. It would seem that Paul has more in mind here than just the giving of gifts to those individuals, but also the giving of those individuals to the church as leaders.

Reread verses 11–13. What are the main tasks of leaders?

_____

_____

_____

_____

_____

How do church leaders know if they are doing what they are supposed to be doing?

_____

_____

_____

_____

Without a doubt, job one for church leaders is equipping the saints to serve. This direct focus should result in the body being edified and everyone moving toward maturity. Much like an athletic coach, church leaders can't measure their success by what they do, but by what others do as a result of their efforts. If the saints (believers) aren't engaged in serving, and the members of the body aren't maturing, then the leaders are not succeeding—no matter how dynamic they are.

When we look at this passage in Ephesians, clearly, the window from which we view spiritual gifts is the window of leaders. The whole subject of spiritual gifts is mentioned, but the emphasis is on the role of leaders and the structure of the body. This is important to keep in mind in understanding specific gifts Paul mentions.

Doctrine

THE WORK OF MINISTRY

The King James Version of the Bible adds a comma in Ephesians 4:12 that many biblical scholars consider misplaced. The first part of the verse reads, *"For the perfecting of the saints, for the work of the ministry. . . ."* The original Greek text has no punctuation, so punctuation in translations is sometimes influenced by the interpretational bias of the translators. In this case, the added comma significantly alters the meaning. Instead of the work of the ministry being what the saints do, the comma makes it what the leaders do. This is possibly a reflection of the hierarchal view of the church that existed in the seventeenth century when the King James Version was translated.

View from a Different Window

I t's amazing to realize that the same object viewed from various angles can appear quite different, depending on which angle you are viewing. For example, I love to snorkel and spearfish. I have learned to appreciate the fact that the same ocean looks entirely different when viewed from above and below the surface. There is beauty in both views, but also very different perspectives. The same approach can be taken when evaluating spiritual gifts. Today, we want to look at the vantage point Peter offers on the subject.

📖 As you look at 1 Peter 4:10–11 in its context (verses 1–11), what is Peter's main point?

_____

_____

_____

_____

_____

_____

Peter makes two assertions in this context that bear directly on the subject of spiritual gifts. First, he reminds us that we ought to be living for the will of God, not the lusts of men (verse 2). Second, he instructs us to be "fervent" in our love for one another. One of the ways we love our brothers and sisters in Christ is when we use our gifts to minister to them. Set against this backdrop, the main point Peter seems to deliver is, "No matter what your gift is, make sure you are being a good steward of it by putting it to work."

Review 1 Peter 4. Which of the three main categories of gifts mentioned in Day One are represented here?

Place all the gifts mentioned here into the categories they most closely fit:

equipping gifts

_____

_____

_____

edifying gifts

_____

_____

_____

evidence gifts

_____

_____

_____

Word Study
WE ARE STEWARDS

The Greek word translated "steward" (*oikonomos*) is where we get our English term "economics." It was a word used to refer to an administrator given charge over the possessions and resources of another. Peter reminds us that we are "stewards" (1 Peter 4:10) of the manifold grace of God given to us.

In 1 Peter 4, we again find two of the three categories mentioned: equipping gifts and edifying gifts. As in Ephesians 4, there is no mention of evidence gifts. The gifts are divided into two main categories of speaking gifts (equipping) and serving gifts (edifying). There is no attempt here to break the two categories down into specific gifts, for Peter's main point is not **how** we serve, but **that** we serve.

Read verses 10–11 once more.

What does verse 10 teach us about the way in which we use our giftedness?

_____

_____

_____

_____

What about verse 11?

_____

_____

_____

_____

In verse 10, we are instructed to be good stewards of the grace given to us. The word "steward" is important here. A steward is one who manages the resources of another. Our gifts are not our own to be used or unused as we see fit, but they belong to God. Therefore, we will answer to Him for what we do with our gifts. In verse 11, we have more specific instructions. If we have a speaking gift, we are to make sure we say what God would say. If we have a serving gift, we are to serve as long as He gives us strength.

What, according to verse 11, is the goal of the gifts?

_____

_____

_____

_____

_____

_____

It is a most grievous sin to usurp the glory of God.

The goal of any and all service is the glory of God. A gift should never be exercised for personal glory. It is a most grievous sin to usurp the glory of God.

We see in today's lesson that Peter's focus differs from that of Paul in Ephesians 4. Paul emphasizes the specific role of leaders (equippers) in helping each of us to serve. Peter's focus is more general. He simply wants all of us to understand that we each have a gift, which is a stewardship entrusted to us by God. We are to put that gift to work (*"employ it"*), whatever it is.

MANY WAYS TO SERVE

Can you imagine what a boring world it would be if everything looked the same? I was struck by this reality the first time I visited Eastern Europe. I began traveling to Poland in the late '80s while it was still a communist country. The people were wonderful, but the country was marked by an appalling sameness. Rows and rows of high–rise apartment complexes in shades of grey were only distinguishable from each other by the numbers on the corners. It seemed as if the whole country had been built from the same set of blueprints. But in 1989, Poland severed ties with the old Soviet Union and moved toward a democratic form of government. A tidal wave of change that was to sweep through Eastern Europe had its beginnings in Poland, and, as a result, it became the first domino to fall in the monumental collapse of the Iron Curtain and the Soviet empire. In my visits to Poland after the fall of communism, I was amazed at the transformation taking place. One of the first changes I noticed was color. Seemingly overnight, buildings were painted in vibrant and varied shades. Variety abounded.

As we look at the body of Christ, it is marked not by sameness, but by amazing beauty and diversity. This seems to be the main point Paul is making in 1 Corinthians 12.

📖 Take a few minutes to read 1 Corinthians 12, keeping this idea of diversity in mind as you read the chapter. Then answer the questions below.

Which of the three primary categories of gifts mentioned in Day One are represented here?

_____

_____

_____

Place all the gifts mentioned here into the categories they most closely fit:

equipping gifts

_____

_____

_____

edifying gifts

_____

_____

_____

evidence gifts

_____

_____

_____

This is the one passage that refers in some form to all three of the categories of gifts. This is not surprising, since Paul's emphasis is on diversity. He actually presents two different lists. The first is in verses 8–10, and the second appears at the end of the chapter in verse 28. Reorganizing these two lists into the three primary categories is not a simple exercise, for it requires interpreting what is meant by unique gifts such as the word of wisdom and the word of knowledge. Some see knowledge and wisdom as related to the functions of equipping gifts such as teaching, prophecy, and exhortation, while others see them as evidence gifts, because those bearing these gifts share supernaturally-revealed information. However, don't let variance of opinion trip you up, for the main thing to see is Paul's emphasis on the variety of the parts of the body. We see the equipping gifts of the apostles, prophets, and teachers mentioned in verse 28. The equipping gift of prophecy is also referred to in verse 10. We see evidence gifts of faith, healings, miracles, distinguishing spirits, tongues and interpretation all listed in verses 9–10, with most of those mentioned again in verse 28. We also see the edifying gifts of helps and administrations in verse 28.

📖 What is the difference in emphasis between the list in verses 8–10 and the list in verse 28?

_____

_____

_____

_____

Verses 8–10, as we saw in the previous lesson, list several groupings of gifts. It would seem that Paul is emphasizing the fact that within the broader categories of service, there are different shades of giftedness. In verse 28, the point seems to be giving a sense of priority and strategy. With the body in view, Paul emphasizes how essential equipping gifts are. This makes a lot of sense in light of Ephesians 4, for it is the equipping gifts that help all the other gifts function effectively. Don't miss one important point though. Before Paul gives us an order of priority for the gifts, he first spends seventeen verses making sure we realize that while certain gifts may be more strategic, they are not any more valuable. He emphatically demonstrates that all gifts are important and are of inestimable value, even if they function differently.

What significant gifts are not mentioned here?

_____

_____

_____

_____

When we look at Paul's wide-ranging list of gifts in 1 Corinthians 12, there are a few gifts mentioned elsewhere that are absent here, such as the gift of mercy or giving. Paul also makes no reference to the equipping gift of the evangelist or pastor. While this is an extensive list, clearly it is not an exhaustive one.

ABIDING SERVICE

W e have looked at three different New Testament passages on the subject of spiritual gifts, and today we will look at a fourth. It is considered by some to be the most significant passage on the subject. In Ephesians, Paul writes to a grounded church. In 1 Corinthians, he writes to a problematic church. But in Romans, Paul writes to a unique church. It is the only letter in the New Testament written to a church that was not founded by an apostle. This explains why Paul spends so much time in Romans focusing on doctrine. The believers there had not benefited from the grounding instruction Paul had given to each of the churches he had helped plant. This concern for doctrine and foundational structure makes the Romans list all the more interesting both for what it includes and for what it does not. Today, we will look at the last passage on gifts and see what else we can learn.

📖 Take a minute to read Romans 12:1–16.

Which of the three main categories of gifts mentioned in day one are represented here?

_____

_____

_____

Place all the gifts mentioned here into the categories they most closely fit:

equipping gifts

_____

_____

_____

_____

edifying gifts

_____

_____

_____

evidence gifts

_____

_____

_____

Unlike the 1 Corinthians list, but in similar fashion to the Ephesians list and Peter's list, Paul gives us only two categories of gifts here: equipping gifts and edifying gifts. The equipping gifts mentioned here are prophecy, teaching, exhortation, and leading. The edifying gifts mentioned here are service, giving, and mercy.

"For through the grace given to me I say to everyone among you not to think more highly of himself than he ought to think; but to think so as to have sound judgment, as God has allotted to each a measure of faith."

Romans 12:3

Read Romans 12:6 again.

What, according to verse 6, determines the particular gift I receive?

_____

_____

How should that affect my attitude about it?

_____

_____

_____

_____

Each of us has a gift. That fact is repeated in each of the four passages. What gift we have is determined by the particular grace given to us. Understanding this should guard us from thinking more highly of ourselves than we ought to (verse 3). Whatever gift we have, it is by God's choice, not through our own efforts. If we are good at something, it is because He has made us good at it.

From what you see in the body as well as in these passages, what are the most commonly found categories of gifts in the four lists?

_____

_____

_____

_____

> **While evidence gifts may manifest themselves at God's discretion, our regular serving is not in the evidence arena.**

It is essential that we notice the pattern of these four passages. Only the 1 Corinthians reference makes mention of evidence gifts. The scant mentioning of evidence gifts by no means diminishes their importance, but it does suggest a very important consideration. More than likely, those gifts are not our primary means of service. It would seem that our day-in and day-out serving of the Lord is done via the equipping gifts or the edifying gifts. While evidence gifts may manifest themselves at God's discretion, our regular serving is not in that arena. For example, the apostle Paul experienced healing and was used to heal others. But most of his service, so far as Scripture records it, was as an apostle/missionary planting churches through teaching the Word.

As you compare all four lists, you should be able to see these categories clearly:

Equipping Gifts (or Speaking Gifts)—Faith/Apostleship, Word of Knowledge/Prophecy, Evangelism, Pastoral/Teaching, Leading.

PURPOSES: **a)** *"For the equipping of the saints for the work of service,* **b)** *to the building up of the body of Christ;* **c)** *until we all attain to the unity of the faith, and of the knowledge of the Son of God, to a mature man, to the measure of the stature which belongs to the fullness of Christ."* (Ephesians 4:12–13)

Edifying Gifts (or Serving Gifts)—Mercy, Word of Wisdom, Giving, Exhortation, Serving/Helps, Administration.

PURPOSES: *"... the work of service"* (Ephesians 4:12), *"... serving one another as good stewards of the manifold grace of God, ... so that in all things God may be glorified through Jesus Christ"* (1 Peter 4:10–11). In other words, the edifying gifts serve in fitting, holding together, and building up the body through the *"proper working of each individual part."* (Ephesians 4:16)

Evidence Gifts (or Sign Gifts)—Gifts of Healings, Effecting Miracles, Distinguishing Spirits, Tongues, Interpretation.

PURPOSES: as a *"sign"* for unbelievers. (1 Corinthians 14:22)

Historically, the equipping and edifying gifts seem to have operated with some consistency. The evidence gifts, however, seem to have surfaced in the body as a whole only at specific points in history. There is a pattern to their emergence as well. In every scriptural occurrence, they are preceded by an extended period of straying and unbelief and followed by a time of new revelation. For example, the miracles of Moses were preceded by the Egyptian enslavement and followed by the giving of the Law. The miraculous dealings of God at the time of David were preceded by the dismal period of the Judges and followed by the writings of David and Solomon. God's miraculous workings in the time of Daniel were preceded by a steady decline in the spirituality of Israel and were followed by the futuristic revelations recorded in the book of Daniel. The mighty moving of God in the time of Christ and the apostles was preceded by four hundred years of silence and spiritual decline and was followed by the writing of the New Testament. The book of Revelation teaches us that the end of the "Laodicean Age" of apostasy will be marked by the miraculous ministry of the two witnesses and will be followed by the revelation of Christ Himself, the Living Word and *"Word made flesh."* (Since this is in quotation marks, shouldn't it have a specific Scripture reference?) Evidence gifts seem to appear only for a short time just prior to God's giving of revelation. This does not mean they are unimportant. They glorify God and manifest His power. However, they should be seen not as an end in themselves, but as a means of drawing attention to God.

FOR ME TO FOLLOW GOD

Each one of us has a spiritual gift. If God lives in us, then He has enabled us to serve and have a ministry. But how do you know what your gift is? An essential element of understanding your spiritual giftedness is recognizing that it is part of who you are. It is not just something you do. If God has gifted you to teach, then you will **want** to teach. If He has gifted you for serving, you will **enjoy** acts of service. If you have the gift of mercy, to show mercy will come as naturally as breathing. Because of this, one way we can take steps to identify our giftedness is to look at what motivates us.

Today, we will consider some indicators to help you determine where your motivations lie, and you may use these indicators to identify your particular area of service. Often our giftedness is accompanied by burdens, desires, and opportunities that coincide with one another. Although you may not be able to answer all of the following questions, reflect carefully and respond to the ones that apply.

Indicator #1
First, think about the people you respect and look up to. Our giftedness will often give us a natural appreciation of certain kinds of ministry more than

others. Gifted people who serve successfully and with impact may attract people of similar giftedness.

 When you think of people serving Christ, whom do you emulate?

_____
_____
_____
_____

INDICATORS OF OUR GIFTEDNESS

- people we respect

- passions

- sense of calling

- desire

- experience

- opportunities

What are their gifts?

_____
_____
_____
_____

If you could be an apprentice under a gifted Christian for special "on-the-job" training in his or her area of giftedness, whom would you choose?

_____

What are his or her gifts?

_____
_____

What type of ministry does he or she perform?

_____
_____

Indicator #2

A second point to consider in identifying our giftedness is our passions. Because our gifts are woven into who we are, we will be passionate in certain corresponding areas. With this in mind, reflect on these questions.

 For what area (or areas) of the Lord's work do you feel burdened?

_____
_____
_____
_____

Is there a particular group for which you have a special concern? (This may move beyond mere giftedness and into your ministry calling.)

Are there any special needs that you consistently notice and help meet?

_____
_____
_____

Indicator #3

A third indicator is your own personal sense of calling. While we may tend to associate that term only with a pastor or missionary, each of us should seek from the Lord a sense of calling to where we fit in the body.

APPLY Is there a specific ministry or area to which you feel called?

_____

_____

_____

What types of gifts will this calling require?

_____

_____

_____

_____

Indicator #4

A fourth indicator is found in the things we desire. We may be conditioned to think that desire is a fleshly motive, but it is not fleshly when we are rightly related to God. If our delight is in Him, our very desires are being molded by Him. We want to do what He calls us to do.

APPLY If you could do anything you wanted to do in serving the Lord, what would it be? (Assume, of course, that this desire is God's will and He has given you the abilities, resources, and opportunities to fulfill this desire.)

_____

_____

_____

_____

If you could do anything you wanted to do in serving the Lord, what would it be?

Although spiritual gifts are given as the Spirit wills, not as we choose, if you could pick your own gifts, what would they be? (Place a number next to your top three in order of preference.)

___ Prophecy ___ Service ___ Teaching ___ Exhortation
___ Giving ___ Leading ___ Mercy

Indicator #5

Another area to consider when trying to discern your giftedness is your past experiences. When you serve where you fit, you ought to sense God's affirmation and feel His pleasure.

APPLY Where have you usually had success or enjoyment when you've served?

_____

_____

_____

_____

Where have you usually failed or been frustrated when serving?

_____

_____

_____

_____

Indicator #6
We want to look at one last indicator of our giftedness: opportunity. God is in charge of our giftedness. He is also in charge of opening the doors for us to serve. We need to look for patterns in the types of opportunities that come our way.

 Where do you find you are often presented with opportunities to serve or the need to serve?

_____

_____

_____

_____

Where are you consistently challenged to serve?

_____

_____

_____

_____

As you consider the six indicators we have looked at today, you may see them begin to line up and point in the same direction. You shouldn't draw a conclusion based on any one indicator; rather, look for a pattern. As you reflect on what you learned this week, why not write out a prayer to the Lord about your own gift.

_____

_____

_____

_____

_____

_____

_____

_____

_____

_____

_____

_____

_____

Notes

The Serving Gifts

(ROMANS 11:33—12:9)

During Jesus' earthly ministry, one event took place that is amazing both for its content and its timing. An argument broke out between the disciples over which of them was the greatest. It's amazing enough that after three years with Jesus, they would debate such a foolish subject, but far more astonishing is the timing of the discussion. It happened the evening before Jesus was crucified, just after He and the disciples had observed the Lord's Supper. Jesus had just revealed that one of them would betray Him, and instead of responding with humility and grief, they quarreled over which of them was the greatest. Incredible! Yet before we rush to judgment, we must realize the same human weaknesses reside in us. We often concern ourselves only with things important to us instead of things that are important to the Lord. In short, we think only of ourselves. Jesus responds to the disciples' debate with a discourse on the nature of leadership.

Jesus contrasts leadership in the kingdom with leadership in the world. *"The kings of the Gentiles,"* He relates, *"lord it over them; and those who have authority over them are called 'Benefactors'"* (Luke 22:25). In other words, to emphasize how important you are is to be just like the world. However, Jesus makes it clear that in the kingdom, things should be different. *"But not so with you,"*

He exclaims, *"but let him who is the greatest among you become as the youngest, and the leader as the servant"* (Luke 22:26). Jesus is contrasting the way the world thinks about leadership and the way the people of God should think. He asks, *"For who is greater, the one who reclines at the table, or the one who serves? Is it not the one who reclines at the table?"* (Luke 22:27a). Clearly this is the way it is in the world. But Jesus is setting up a new paradigm. He is redefining leadership by His own example: *"But I am among you as the one who serves"* (Luke 22:27b).

Jesus' words were far more than mere religious hyperbole. They were backed by His actions. John's gospel confirms that before this conversation even took place, Jesus had washed the disciples' feet. We tend to make an example out of this, but we often miss the fact that He was meeting a real need. In that culture, where walking in sandaled feet on dusty roads was the norm, foot washing was more than just symbolic. The lesson is not in what was done, but in who did it. The greatest person in the room performed a task reserved for the least important. In so doing, Jesus made valuable the service of the lowliest servant (lowliest in the eyes of the world, that is). He said with His actions, "This is important."

The Serving Gifts | **DAY ONE**

PUTTING THE GIFTS INTO PERSPECTIVE

For far too long, the Church has defined leadership more like the world defines it instead of the way Christ defines it. Often we are like the disciples, arguing (if not verbally, then mentally) over who is the greatest. Yet, from God's perspective, serving is the most important thing we can do. As I look at the body of Christ, I see gifts of mercy and service (helps) in greater abundance than any other gifts. The world views these gifts as common, but I think a different explanation can be offered. God supplies those gifts in greater abundance because they are more necessary. We think that churches will shut down without a pastor, and sometimes they do. But God knows that churches will grind to a halt without the gifts of service and mercy, regardless of their leadership. Certainly, all spiritual gifts are needed in a church, including those of leadership and administration, but it's time we started viewing them from God's perspective.

As we saw last week, four passages in the New Testament address the subject of spiritual gifts. In three of those passages (Romans 12:1–16; Ephesians 4:11–13; 1 Peter 4:10–11), only the equipping and edifying gifts are mentioned. Evidence gifts are omitted; however, that does not suggest that they are unbiblical. It does suggest that the way we serve God day-in and day-out is primarily through equipping and edifying gifts. Today's lesson will be centered on the Romans passage, since it provides the most thorough explanation regarding these two gift categories. We will look more closely at individual gifts in the next two lessons, but for now we will focus on the edifying gifts of **service, giving,** and **mercy.** In order for us to fully appreciate what the passage in Romans says about these gifts, it is important to understand the context. We will see how Paul sets the stage for teaching the Romans about spiritual gifts.

📖 Read Romans 11:33–36 and reflect on its message as it relates to the subject of spiritual gifts.

_____

_____

_____

_____

Before Paul addresses the subject of gifts, he reminds us of the One who gave us our gifts. It is important to keep in mind the depths *"of the riches of the wisdom and knowledge of God"* when we reflect on whatever particular gift He has given us. Often we are guilty of wanting to "counsel" the Lord on what He should have given us instead of trusting His wisdom.

📖 How does the message of Romans 12:1–2 relate to the subject of spiritual gifts?

_____

_____

_____

_____

Chapter 12 begins with the word *"therefore,"* indicating a transition. In this case the transition moves us into one of the most specific application passages of the entire book. In verse 3, Paul, introduces the subject of gifts, but an application of the principles found in verses 1 and 2 must come before we will be able to identify and live out our giftedness. We must surrender ourselves to Him and His service before we can confidently know how He has gifted us. We cannot look at our giftedness through the eyes of the world, for the world will only value those things that draw attention to us.

📖 According to verse 3, how does thinking more highly than one ought and thinking with sound judgment relate to the topic of gifts?

_____

_____

_____

_____

With certain gifts comes the danger of spiritual pride. Yet if we truly understand the idea of a gift, there can be no pride. We did nothing to earn it, and we cannot take credit for it. We can only be humbly grateful that God invites us to join Him as He works. The opposite of this verse is true as well—sound judgment would also preclude thinking "more lowly" of ourselves than we should.

What is implied by the statement in verse 3, *"God has allotted to each a measure of faith"*?

_____

_____

_____

_____

Word Study
PRESENT

The Greek Word translated "present" in Romans 12:1 (*paristano*) means "to stand before." It was used of a soldier who would report to his commanding officer to receive orders. It carries the idea of placing oneself at another's disposal.

Did You Know?
UTILIZING YOUR GIFTS

The phrase *"let each exercise them accordingly"* is in italic type in most Bibles. The italic typeface indicates that the phrase doesn't actually appear in the original Greek manuscripts, but that the translators saw this idea implied in the verse's construction. The concept of Christians individually utilizing their gifts seems to be supported by the admonitions in the verses that follow.

That God *"has allotted"* to each of us a *"measure of faith"* indicates that along with our spiritual gift we are also given the ability to trust God as He uses us in our area of service. The fact that we have a *"measure"* of faith suggests that we do not have all faith for all gifts. God enables us to trust Him in our particular area of giftedness. In verse 6, Paul tells us that our gifts differ *"according to the grace given to us."* Where God guides, He provides. For the task He calls us to, He also enables us.

THE GIFT OF SERVICE

Perhaps the most abundant gift in the body of Christ today is the gift of service, or as the King James Version translates it, the gift of "ministry." This gift is widely distributed because it is greatly needed. The Greek word translated "service" (*diakonia*) is where we get our English term "deacon." This doesn't mean that everyone with this gift should be a deacon, or that every deacon in a church is required to have this gift. There is a difference between the gift of serving and the office of deacon. Just as one can seek the qualities of an elder without seeking to be one, so can one have the gift of serving and use it in varying capacities. *Diakonia* carries the idea of practical service. It is used in the New Testament many different ways. The meaning can and should be interpreted very broadly—any kind of practical service. This gift is administered primarily through meeting physical needs, not spiritual ones. But the use of the gift of service makes it possible to meet spiritual needs. Today, we'll look at several places in Scripture where the service gift is put into practice. Through this process, we will gain a better understanding of how the service gift is to function within the body of Christ.

📖 Read Luke 10:38–42, where the Greek word for service is used, and answer the questions below.

What was Martha obsessing about?

_____

_____

What does this reveal about the potential dangers of the gift of service?

_____

_____

_____

_____

Doctrine

SERVICE OVERKILL

"Only a few things are necessary, really only one" (Luke 10:42). Many have interpreted this passage to mean that only one thing matters, to sit at Jesus' feet. However, this would mean that the gift of service did not matter. It's possible Jesus was saying "only a few dishes are necessary, really only one." Martha was not wrong for serving, but for being excessive in her service and neglecting the opportunity to spend time with Jesus.

The Greek root word for service, *diakonos,* is used twice in this passage. The first time, it is used to speak of Martha being distracted with *"all her preparations."* Here the idea refers to the practical task of preparing a meal. This root word is used once again to describe Martha rebuking her sister for leaving her *"to do all the serving"* alone. Here, the word conveys Martha's preparations of the meal. It also implies that she was not wrong to serve but was wrong to judge others based on her gift. She also let her serving interfere with listening to Jesus' words.

📖 Look at Acts 6:1–4. The same root word for service (*diakonos*) used in Luke 10:38–42 is used in Acts 6:1 ("*the daily serving of food*") and again in verse 2 ("*to serve tables*"). What does this suggest about how this gift functions?

_____

_____

_____

_____

In Acts 6, we see that there was a need for the widows to be fed, but it would be ineffective to have church leaders tied up doing that. Instead, they asked the congregation to appoint people who could take charge of this task. An important point to recognize here is that the service of these men makes it possible for the leaders to devote themselves to prayer and the ministry of the Word as they should. Although the task is a physical one, it has a spiritual result. Traditionally, the men that were chosen by the Jerusalem church are called the first deacons, though at this point in the development of the Church, it is doubtful that an official position of "deacon" had been created.

📖 Another biblical example of this gift would be Tabitha (Dorcas) of Acts 9:36 and 39. Examine what is taught in these verses by her example regarding the gift of service.

_____

_____

_____

_____

Although this passage does not use the word "service," clearly this gift is reflected in the function of Dorcas' ministry. We are told that she was "*abounding with deeds of kindness and charity, which she continually did.*" Specifically, it appears she had a ministry of making tunics and garments and giving them to widows and the needy. As a believer, she took the skills that she had and put them to use in serving others by meeting practical needs. This is what the gift of service is all about.

📖 How, according to 1 Peter 4:11, do you exercise the gift of service?

_____

_____

_____

_____

Peter tells us that whoever serves is to do so "*as one who is serving by the strength which God supplies.*" In other words, "do it as you have strength to do so." We are not to serve to the neglect of ourselves or other priorities or responsibilities, but only as God enables us to do so. The net result of such serving is that "*in all things God may be glorified through Jesus Christ, to whom belongs the glory and dominion forever and ever.*"

Obviously, the gift of service is an important gift. It meets spiritual needs by meeting physical and practical needs.

THE GIFT OF GIVING

Next in our list of **edifying** gifts is the gift of **giving.** This gift is often confused and misrepresented. It comes from the Greek word *metadidomi*, from *meta*, meaning "with" (referring to association), and *didomi*, meaning "to give." *Metadidomi* is concerned not just with giving, but with all things associated with giving. Generally, the Greek word means to communicate or impart or share one's own possessions, but the gift can also function in overseeing the distribution of a church's benevolence. It is the divine enablement to financially help those in need. Accompanied by discernment, it is the ability to detect needs and to discern between true and false needs. A person with this gift gives without looking back, without second thoughts, without regret. One doesn't have to be wealthy to have this gift, nor does it imply that all wealthy people have it. Also, those not having this gift are in no way excused from being generous. Generosity is a trait all Christians should have, regardless of our giftedness.

📖 In Luke 3:11, *metadidomi* is translated "share." Look up this verse; note its context; and reflect on its teaching about the gift of giving.

_____

_____

_____

Luke 3:11 shows us some of the teachings of John the Baptist. He had just instructed his listeners to bear *"fruits in keeping with repentance"* (Luke 3:8). When the crowd asked for specific examples, he told them, *"Let the man who has two tunics share with him who has none; and let him who has food do likewise."* This is significant in that it shows that giving is not simply about money. Those with a surplus are to share with those who have none. While all of us are called to be givers, some are uniquely gifted for this task.

📖 In Ephesians 4:28, once again, *metadidomi* is translated "share." Look up this verse; read its context; and reflect on its teaching about the gift of giving.

_____

_____

_____

Here in Ephesians, we see that we are not to steal (to be a taker), but that we are to work with our hands on something worthwhile or beneficial. This will enable us to meet not only our own needs, but will create a surplus to meet the needs of others. We are to be ready to "share" with those who are in need. Again, we see that the needy are to be the focus of the gift of giving.

📖 Looking at Romans 12:8, identify how Paul says the gift of giving is to be exercised. Then reflect on what you think this verse means.

_____

_____

_____

"Let the man who has two tunics share with him who has none; and let him who has food do likewise."

Luke 3:11

Paul points out here that one with the gift of giving is to exercise it with "liberality." The Greek word here doesn't mean generously, but rather conveys the idea of sincerity or having no ulterior motives. There is an inherent danger with the gift of giving. It is one of the easiest gifts to misuse. When we give, people are naturally grateful, but if we aren't careful, our motives in giving can appear questionable. We cannot give in the biblical sense and have strings attached to our gifts. We cannot give with the expectation of special attention or favors in return. We must give as unto the Lord.

📖 Read Matthew 6:1–4 and write down what you learn about the right and wrong way to give.

_____

_____

_____

_____

In the Sermon on the Mount, Jesus gave instruction on the use and misuse of giving, as well as other spiritual disciplines. In verse 1, He warns us against *"practicing . . . righteousness before men to be noticed by them."* If we do so, we forfeit any reward from God. When we give, we are not to draw attention to our giving, or else the attention we get will be our only reward. God must be the audience of this gift—He is the one to be pleased by it.

A good biblical example of the gift of giving would be Joseph of Arimathea. We are told in Matthew's gospel that he was *"a rich man"* (Matthew 27:57) who owned a tomb hewn out of solid rock (see Matthew 27:60) that had never been used (see John 19:41). Such a burial place was a luxury few could afford. Yet Joseph gave it to house the body of Jesus. Being a believer (see John 19:38), Joseph took from his own resources and purchased the linen cloth used as the burial shroud (see Mark 15:46), and, along with Nicodemas the Pharisee, provided the burial spices. Together, they prepared the body of Jesus for a proper and honorable burial. Joseph used his own material resources to be a blessing to the Lord.

Did You Know?

? **GIVING DISCREETLY**

During Jesus' time on earth, one of the formal Jewish places to give was at the local synagogue. Large brass pots with trumpet-shaped mouths were placed strategically around the Temple and used for collecting monetary donations for the poor. As Jesus states in Matthew 6:1–4, some drew attention to themselves and their gift by tossing large amounts of small-denomination coins into the pots, making as much noise as possible. The principle Christ teaches is that we are not to draw attention to ourselves and our gifts.

THE GIFT OF MERCY

The Serving Gifts **DAY FOUR**

The last **edifying** gift we encounter in Paul's list in Romans 12 is the gift of **mercy.** The Greek word *eleeo*, translated "mercy," means "an inner emotion leading to outward manifestations of pity." It carries the idea of showing mercy, showing compassion, and extending help for the consequence of sin. The general meaning is to have compassion or mercy on a person experiencing undesirable circumstances. Mercy implies not only a feeling of sympathy for the misfortunes of others but also an active desire to remove those miseries. It assumes a need on the part of the recipient and adequate resources on the part of the giver. This ministry involves giving to those who need pity, not just donating resources or money. This is direct personal ministry to those in need—the gift of sympathy. A person endowed with the gift of mercy is moved to do something about the misery of others—cards, notes, hugs, tears, and so forth.

As you look at Romans 12:8, identify the instruction Paul gives to the one with this gift.

_____

_____

_____

_____

The gift of mercy is to be exercised *"with cheerfulness."* The Greek word conveys the idea of happiness, joy, and gladness. In other words, as we show mercy toward the misfortunes of others, we are not to allow their circumstances to rob us of our joy. We are not merely to empathize, but we are also to encourage.

Look up Matthew 23:23 and write down what you read about the importance of mercy.

_____

_____

_____

_____

As with all the edifying gifts, there is the potential danger of not seeing the gift of mercy as being very important. Yet, in this verse, Jesus calls it one of the *"weightier provisions of the law."* In 2 Corinthians 1:3, our Lord is called *"the Father of mercies."* Clearly, to Him, mercy is an issue of great significance.

What does God's mercy, as reflected in Titus 3:5, teach us about the functioning of the gift of mercy?

_____

_____

_____

_____

In Titus 3:5, we are reminded that our salvation is not based on *"deeds which we have done in righteousness,"* but rather is *"according to His mercy."* One of the fundamental attributes of mercy is that it does not try to assess guilt or responsibility for the misfortunes in which people find themselves. If mercy must be earned or deserved, then it really isn't mercy at all.

What does James 3:17 have to say about mercy?

_____

_____

_____

_____

"The wisdom from above is . . . full of mercy"

James 3:17

In James 3:17 we are given a description of *"the wisdom from above."* One of the attributes of divine wisdom is that it is *"full of mercy."* When we show mercy to others, we are aligning ourselves with the heart of God.

Jesus gives us an example of the gift of mercy. When questioned by a lawyer about the requirements of eternal life, He affirmed the "Great Commandment," to *"love the Lord your God with all your heart, and with all your soul, and with all your strength, and with all your mind; and your neighbor as yourself"* (Luke 10:27). When the lawyer, looking for a loophole, asks, *"Who is my neighbor?"* (Luke 10:29), Jesus responded with what we commonly call the parable of the "good Samaritan." Jesus tells us that when this Samaritan encountered the Jewish man who had been beaten, *"he felt compassion"* (Luke 10:33). After bandaging the injured man's wounds, this good Samaritan spent the night caring for him and even hired an innkeeper to care for his needs after that. Though two very distinguished men declined to help the injured man before the Samaritan arrived, we have the proclamation of the inquiring lawyer that the Samaritan was *"the one who showed mercy"* (Luke 10:37). Mercy is not just meeting physical needs; it is meeting emotional needs as well.

FOR ME TO FOLLOW GOD

The body of Christ is not a box filled with identical parts, but it is an intricate gathering of very different parts working together under the direction of the Designer. You see, we all have different gifts and strengths and abilities. Like snowflakes in winter, all of us are unique patterns of beauty, yet seldom do we look closely enough at each other to appreciate that fact. The truth that I have at least one spiritual gift guarantees that the body needs me. It is tangible proof that, like the complicated inner workings of a watch, no matter how small a part I play, I am needed to fulfill the designer's plan. Another truth is that I don't have all the gifts. I am not complete in and of myself, nor did God ever intend me to be. *"We, who are many, are one body in Christ, and individually members one of another"* (Romans 12:5).

As you reflect on what Romans teaches about spiritual gifts, it will be helpful to review some of the key issues of the context of this list of gifts. This week, we want to concentrate thinking rightly about our gifts. Perhaps the best place to start is with a right understanding of the source of your spiritual giftedness.

📖 Take a few minutes to reread Romans 11:33–36 and consider the evaluation questions that follow.

 Have you ever struggled with the way God gifted you (or didn't gift you)?

_____

_____

What message stands out to you from this passage in Romans about trusting how God made you?

_____

_____

_____

"Oh, the depth of the riches both of the wisdom and knowledge of God! How unsearchable are His judgments and unfathomable His ways!"

Romans 11:33

Perhaps you struggle in a different way. Maybe you think you deserve the credit for your giftedness. What do verses 35 and 36 say regarding this attitude?

_____

_____

_____

_____

We learn from
Romans 12:1–2 that
God's will for our
giftedness is "good,
acceptable, and
perfect."

Romans 12:1–2 is a familiar passage to most of us, yet you may never have really considered its message in light of the discussion of spiritual gifts that follows. These first two verses reveal to us how we can "prove what the will of God is." We learn here that God's will for our giftedness is "good, acceptable, and perfect." We also learn some of the things we must do before we can see that realized. As you consider the steps listed in this passage, check the ones you feel you've effectively completed on discerning your spiritual giftedness.

 Have you surrendered yourself to the Lord completely to be used however He desires?

_____

_____

Have you set aside the world's values as they relate to your giftedness and dedicated yourself to using it for those things that really matter in life?

_____

_____

Are you staying in the Word of God to gain His perspective on your giftedness and using it to serve Him?

_____

_____

In light of the challenge of Romans 12:3, as you reflect on your own struggles in determining how God has gifted you, where would you place yourself on the spectrum below?

Thinking   Thinking   Thinking
Too   Rightly   Too
Highly   Lowly

📖 Look over Romans 12:4–6 and consider the evaluation questions that follow.

_____

_____

_____

Do you ever struggle with "tunnel vision," thinking that everyone should have the same values, gifts, and service traits that you have or that your gifts are the only ones that really matter?

Do you ever struggle with being too independent and miss out on meeting your need to network with other believers as part of a whole?

_____

_____

Are you content with the "grace" allotted to you?

_____

_____

Close out this week's lesson by writing a prayer to the Lord that gives all these issues to Him.

_____

_____

_____

_____

_____

_____

_____

_____

_____

_____

_____

_____

_____

_____

_____

_____

_____

_____

Notes

The Speaking Gifts

(ROMANS 12:3–8)

Countless bones make up the framework of the human body. You could probably name some of them. I'm told the cranium is the densest of all human bones, and the bone that runs from the hip to the knee, the femur, is the longest bone. But, do you know what the smallest human bones are? There are three of them, and they are located in your middle ear: the malleus, the incus, and the stapes. The proper alignment of these three bones makes hearing possible. One of the most innovative and life-altering surgeries in medicine today is a "stapedectomy." This operation repairs and realigns the largest of these bones. I was fascinated to hear a firsthand account of one of these operations. A man who had been deaf for twenty-six years had his hearing restored through this surgery. When he heard his own voice for the first time in many years, tears began streaming down his face and he exclaimed, "Why, that's me! That's *my* voice I hear!"

Can you imagine what it would feel like to hear for the first time in twenty-six years? It's easy to take the miracle of speaking and hearing for granted. Yet our lives are dramatically shaped by this marvel of communication. We are able to be instructed and to learn. We are able to grow and develop. The dramatic biography of Helen Keller gives testimony to the hindrances and

Through the ministry of the speaking gifts, we are all equipped to walk with the Lord and serve Him effectively.

challenges one who cannot speak or hear faces. In the body of Christ, our Lord has gifted certain individuals with the ability to speak His truth in ways that benefit the whole body. We call these gifts the "speaking gifts." Through their use, all of us are equipped to walk with the Lord and serve Him effectively. Four gifts mentioned in the book of Romans are categorized as speaking gifts: prophecy, teaching, exhortation, and leadership. Each of these gifts plays an important role in the life of the body of Christ. This week we will spend one day studying each of these spiritual gifts, and we will learn what they mean and how they are to function in ministry.

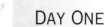

DAY ONE

THE GIFT OF PROPHECY

Today there are some who claim to be "modern day" prophets, possessing the ability to tell the future. They make predictions, often of a vague or general nature, and most are forgotten. But what if one of their predictions comes true? Does this validate them and what they have to say? Is this what the gift of prophecy is all about? The Law has specific instructions regarding those who claim to predict the future. In Deuteronomy 13, we are told that if a prophet's words come true but he counsels the people to follow other gods, he is to be put to death. In Deuteronomy 18, we are instructed that if the words of a prophet don't come true, he is not to be feared. I once read about a conference where one of the speakers claimed to have the highest percentage of correct prophecies of any of the modern day, so-called prophets. According to the Bible, if that percentage is anything less than one hundred percent, then he's no prophet at all! But is this really what the gift of prophecy is all about? I don't think so.

When we hear the word "prophecy," we often think of Old Testament prophets who spoke for God. Perhaps the most dramatic aspect of the Old Testament prophet's work was to reveal and disclose the unfolding of God's plan for the future. Prophecy as a spiritual gift shares some similarities with the ministry of the Old Testament prophet, but we need to guard against equating the two. The ministry of the Old Testament prophet functioned differently because it was not supported by the full canon of Scripture. Although we generally associate the Old Testament prophet with telling the future, that was not his primary ministry. Prophecy in both the Old and New Testament involves two things: **a) foretelling**—predicting events before they happen, and **b) forthtelling**—speaking the mind, will, and perspective of God to His people and pointing out deviations from His way. When you look at the Bible as a whole, forthtelling is the primary exercise of prophecy. The foretelling dimension was rare in the Old Testament, and is even more rare in the New Testament.

Did You Know?

THE GIFT OF PROPHECY

The gift of prophecy functions in two different dimensions:

■ foretelling—revealing the future

■ forthtelling—revealing the perspective of God

📖 Read 1 Corinthians 14:1–5 and write down everything these verses say or imply about the ministry of the gift of prophecy.

_____

_____

_____

_____

_____

One of the things that stands out in this passage is that gifts are to be desired earnestly, especially the gift of prophecy. We should not take this passage to mean that we can select a particular gift we desire, for Paul has already made it clear in 1 Corinthians 12:11 that the Spirit distributes our gifts *"as He wills,"* not as we choose. More likely, the point is that we should desire to see prophecy exercised in our churches, for we see in verse 3 that the ministry of prophecy results in *"edification and exhortation and consolation."* One who prophesies builds up the church (verse 4). This paints a different picture of the gift of prophecy than the contemporary idea that prophets are eccentric types who are harsh and short with their words.

📖 Read 1 Corinthians 14:22–25 and 31 and record your observations on how prophecy ministers to others.

_____

_____

_____

One way prophecy ministers is to the unbeliever. Here, through the working of the gift of prophecy, the unbeliever is convicted and called to account. His heart is reached. Verse 31 tells us that through this ministry of prophecy, all may learn and be exhorted. To summarize, it appears that the primary working of this gift is in personalizing the message for the audience. The prophet is able to relate the Word of God to listeners in a personal way that moves them to action.

📖 Examine Romans 12:6 and make note of what you read concerning how the gift of prophecy is to function.

_____

_____

_____

_____

_____

As you look at Romans 12:6, some knowledge of the Greek language will be helpful to you. First, the verse literally reads, "And having gifts differing according to the grace given to us, whether prophecy, according to the proportion of one's faith." Obviously, the idea of exercising our giftedness is implied, but the part of the text that directly addresses this idea should be in italic type in your Bible, indicating the translators added those words. (See lesson 5 side note on page 65 pertaining to Romans 12:6) One important observation: there is no personal pronoun in the original Greek before the word faith. However, a definite article is found in the original Greek, and the New American Standard Bible translators took this article to mean *"his faith"* or "one's faith." A more direct translation, however, would be *"the faith."* The difference is thus: the definite article in Greek makes the meaning of the verse more specific; therefore the question here is, "What meaning does the verse specify?" Most likely, it is not pointing to how much faith prophets should have, but to their knowledge of the whole of Christian doctrine and how their "faith" lines up with it. Prophets are responsible for making sure their message is God's word, not their own.

📖 Look up 1 Corinthians 13:8–10.

What happens to the gift of prophecy?

_____

_____

_____

When Paul says, *"when the perfect comes,"* what does he mean?

_____

_____

_____

This passage clearly teaches that the gift of prophecy, along with tongues and knowledge, will one day cease. There is universal agreement on this point. However, there is no agreement on exactly when this will happen. Some believe it has already ceased, while others see it as a gift still functioning today. The key revolves around how you interpret the phrase *"when the perfect comes."* Those who argue that the gift of prophecy in the traditional sense no longer exists usually believe that the "perfect" came when the New Testament was completed. But if you follow the flow of logic through the context of this verse, the use of the terms "now" and "then" (particularly in verse 12), indicates that *"the perfect"* will come when we see Jesus *"face to face."*

It seems pretty clear from Romans 12 that the gift of prophecy is alive and well in some form. Some argue that the **foretelling** dimension is not active today, but there is no reason to conclude that the **forthtelling** function is also inoperative in this modern era. Some see this gift as something akin to a gift of preaching. I believe the gift of prophecy spoken of in Romans 12 should be viewed as relevant to any speaking ministry, both to small and large groups.

Some have suggested that the apostle Peter had the gift of prophecy, and if this is true, we see both the strengths and weaknesses of this gift in his life. He had the discernment of a prophet, for it was Peter who rightly perceived that Jesus was the Messiah (see Matthew 16:16). But he also confronted Christ when he did not fully understand, and, at one point, he actually tried to rebuke Jesus concerning the cross (see Matthew 16:22). The prophet has discernment, but he must be sure he has heard from God before he speaks or he may be swayed by his own opinions.

The Speaking Gifts   DAY TWO

THE GIFT OF TEACHING

One of the most significant stories in the book of Acts is the birth of the first church composed entirely of Gentiles. It was located in Antioch, and its beginnings can be traced directly to the persecution that began with the stoning of Stephen. Acts 11:19–30 tells us that those scattered by the persecution made their way through different parts of Asia, speaking the Word to Jews. But some who came to Antioch began speaking to the Greeks as well. The response of these Gentiles was immediate and significant. A *"large number"* turned to the Lord. This presented a dilemma for the mother church in Jerusalem, for the people of that congregation weren't quite sure what to do with a Gentile church. They hadn't planned for a seismic shift of this magnitude, so they sent one of their most trusted leaders, Barnabas, to check things out. Once Barnabas arrived, he *"witnessed the grace of God"* and affirmed this new work. While he was there, even more people turned to the Lord. It is significant that believers were first called "Christians" at Antioch. Next, they turned their attention to what should be done with this newly formed church—so many new converts with so many needs. Verses 25 and 26 tell us, *"And he* [Barnabas] *left for Tarsus to look for Saul; and when he had found him, he brought him to Antioch."* Why would Barnabas need Saul (later known as the apostle Paul; see Acts 13:9)? The answer to this question is significant not just for Antioch, but for us today. At the end of Acts 11:26 we are told, *"And it came about that for an entire year they met with the church, and taught considerable numbers."* When Barnabas arrived in Antioch, *"considerable numbers were brought to the Lord"* (Acts 11:24). When Paul showed up, considerable numbers were taught. I suspect Barnabas already recognized that Paul possessed the gift of teaching, and he also discerned that this was exactly what was needed at Antioch.

The mission of the Church throughout the ages is not just evangelism, as important as that is. The Great Commission (see Matthew 28:18–20) is not just to make converts of all nations, but to *"make disciples."* Teaching is a critical need in the Church. While evangelism brings new life, teaching sustains that new life. All of us are able to study the Scriptures and learn, but there are certain ones God has placed among us who are specially gifted not just to understand the Bible, but to communicate what it says in a way that all can understand. Paul was such a man—and thus it's no small wonder that he wrote nearly half of the New Testament—letters that still instruct us today. God still gifts individuals in this way today, and their work is essential to the ongoing ministry of the body of Christ. Today, we will look specifically at the gift of **teaching.** Those with this gift serve to give **instruction**—they possess the supernatural ability to unfold the Word of God so that people can grasp its meaning. The ability to teach the Word doesn't come from training (such as seminary courses) or natural ability, but it is a supernatural endowment that fuels both the desire to study and understand the Word and the ability to communicate it clearly. While training can make one more effective at teaching, it cannot impart the gift of teaching, which comes only from God.

📖 Look at Colossians 1:28 and 1 Timothy 4:15–16 and write what you learn there about what makes an effective teacher.

_____

_____

_____

In Colossians 1:28, we learn that teaching requires wisdom, and the goal of teaching is the maturation of the audience. Paul advises in 1 Timothy 4:15–16 that teachers must pay close attention to their teaching. The implication of effort is underscored by the call to *"persevere"* and the admonitions to *"take pains"* and to *"be absorbed."* The audience ought to see the teacher's efforts in preparation and study.

📖 Take a look at Romans 2:17–24 and answer the questions that follow.

What must one do to be able to teach (verse 18)?

_____

_____

_____

What are teachers able to do with what they have learned (verse 19)?

_____

_____

_____

What is the tool used by teachers (verse 20)?

_____

_____

What is the result if teachers' lives don't match their instruction?

_____

_____

_____

_____

Some important distinctions are made here about the proper functioning of the gift of teaching. First, teaching begins with knowing and being instructed in the Scriptures (verse 18). The one who knows then is able to guide and enlighten others (verse 19). We see in verse 20 that the Scriptures, being the *"embodiment"* of knowledge and truth, are the only valid tool of the teacher and that they are useful to correct the foolish and to teach the immature. But most importantly, we see that teachers are accountable to live out what they instruct others to do. Verse 24 shows us that it is possible to speak truth with our lips and to speak lies with our lives (blasphemies—untruths about God). To be effective, there must be consistency between what teachers say and how they live.

📖 As we saw at the beginning of today's lesson, the apostle Paul probably had the gift of teaching. Look at the advice he gives to one of his key disciples in 1 Timothy 1:3–7, and make note of what you learn about effective teaching.

_____

_____

_____

_____

_____

_____

Paul's counsel to his disciple, Timothy, offers us important guidelines for effective teaching. The first is perhaps not so obvious. Yet in counseling Timothy to stay at Ephesus so that he could instruct others not to teach *"strange doctrines,"* Paul teaches us that one of the proper functions of a teacher is to help others separate truth from error. We thus can gather from Paul's advice the kinds of things that lead a teacher into error: paying attention to myths, speculations, and fruitless discussions. We also glean two more important guidelines. First, all teaching should have as its goal a heart of love. In other words, instruction should affect the lifestyle of the audience. Second, teachers cannot effectively teach until they understand the material they are teaching (verse 7).

📖 What do you learn from 2 Timothy 2:24–26 about effective teaching?

_____

_____

_____

_____

Here we learn much about the manner of successful teachers. To communicate truth effectively, one cannot have an argumentative nature. Instead, teachers should use kindness, patience, and gentleness. This does not mean teachers should sacrifice truth, for their job does involve correcting those in error. More than anything else, this passage seems to emphasize that effective teachers have an eye on their audience and their own teaching method, not just on the content of their teaching.

Not everyone who teaches has the gift of teaching. In 1 Timothy 3:2, Paul indicates that every elder must be *"able to teach,"* but this does not mean that all elders have that gift. The pure gift of teaching is focused mainly on instruction. Those with this gift have a passion for study, and they like to share what they learn. If they have a weakness, it may be that they share too much information. However, teachers of God's Word should always guard the truths found there.

Did You Know?

PAUL, TIMOTHY, AND EPHESUS

Paul wrote the books of 1 and 2 Timothy to his disciple, Timothy while Timothy was in a position of leadership in the church at Ephesus. Paul had originally planted the church at Ephesus, and Apollos had been its main leader then. Timothy was now leading this church when Paul wrote these letters to him. Later, the apostle John would lead this significant church.

THE GIFT OF EXHORTATION

The Speaking Gifts **DAY THREE**

Exhortation is not a word we often use anymore except in Christian circles. It is probably just as well, for apart from the Lord, exhortation is an empty exercise. The word "exhortation" comes from the Greek term *paraklesis* (from *para,* "alongside," and *kaleo,* "to call"), meaning to come alongside someone and call or charge him. The Greek word is used in several different ways in the New Testament. It is used to call upon someone to do something, to comfort someone, to encourage, to admonish, and even to invite. The basic concept is to **beseech** or comfort, to come to one's side as a helper or advocate. The dominant idea is **encouragement**—encouraging people to act on God's Word, to obey. Prophecy is aimed at the will; teaching is aimed at the understanding, but the ministry of **exhortation** is aimed at the heart, encouraging the fainthearted. Perhaps the clearest biblical example of this gift is found in the person of Barnabas. He is best known as a mentor to the apostle Paul. You may not be aware that Barnabas wasn't really his name, but his nickname. It means "son of encouragement," and his life was certainly characterized by this attribute. When he arrived at Antioch and affirmed that this new church was a work of God, we are told that he *"began to encourage them all with resolute heart to remain true to the Lord."* Barnabas was exhortation personified. He came alongside the apostle Paul shortly after his conversion and encouraged him when no one else would (see Acts 9:27), and he brought Paul on board as an apprentice in his work at Antioch (see Acts 11:25). He had a similar relationship of mentoring and encouragement in the life of Mark, author of the gospel that bears his name (see Acts 15:36-41). People endowed with the gift of exhortation make excellent disciplers, mentors, and counselors. The gift of exhortation is a Word-based gift.

Word Study

EXHORT

The Greek word translated "exhort" is the term *paraklesis* (from *para,* "alongside," and *kaleo,* "to call"), meaning to come alongside someone and call or charge that person. This same root word is applied to the Holy Spirit in John 14:16 where He is called the *"Helper"* or *"Comforter."* In the Trinity, God the Father is the leader and prophet. Jesus is the teacher. He is called the "Word" ("message" or "logic") of God in John 1. The Holy Spirit is the exhorter.

Look up the following verses and record what you learn about exhortation.

Acts 13:15

_____

_____

_____

_____

1 Timothy 4:13

_____

_____

_____

_____

2 Timothy 4:2

_____

_____

_____

_____

In Acts 13:15, we see exhortation following the reading of the Law and the Prophets. The emphasis is on explaining and applying what the audience has just heard. In 1 Timothy 4:13, we again see exhortation listed along with teaching as accompaniment to the public reading of Scripture. The implication is that exhortation is one of the pulpit functions. It is one form of preaching. The gift of exhortation can be used in other settings of course, but the pulpit is one of the places it should be used. In 2 Timothy 4:2, Paul gives us a list of the many different faces of preaching the Word of God. Preaching includes reproof, rebuke, exhortation, and instruction.

📖 Examine Titus 1:9 and write down what stands out to you regarding the correct way to exhort. Also write down any potential mistakes this verse reveals.

_____

_____

_____

_____

In describing the role of elders, Paul points out that one facet of their ministry is to _"exhort in sound doctrine."_ This reveals a potential danger in the gift of exhortation. Because an exhorter is motivated by practicality and application, he may put his emphasis there, to the neglect of doctrine. An exhorter can be an entertaining speaker even when he has nothing to say. To be balanced, he must be sure to develop the scriptural content of his message adequately.

📖 You will also want to look at the following instances where exhortation is evidenced and identify how it usually operates.

". . . holding fast the faithful word which is in accordance with the teaching, so that he will be able both to exhort in sound doctrine and to refute those who contradict."

Titus 1:9

1 Corinthians 4:16

_____

_____

_____

_____

1 Thessalonians 4:1

_____

_____

_____

_____

1 Peter 5:1

_____

_____

_____

_____

The message of 1 Corinthians 4:16 is one of application. Paul charges the Corinthian church members to act. In 1 Thessalonians 4:1, Paul gives us a good example of exhortation in action. He calls the believers in Thessalonica to diligently apply what they had been taught. Again, we see the emphasis on application. In 1 Peter 5:1, we see Peter use this same word (**exhort**— from _parakaleo_) to address his fellow elders and charge them to activity.

Exhortation is not satisfied with truth for the sake of information. The gift of exhortation is motivated by application. The exhorter, like Barnabas, is a cheerleader and coach. One with this gift takes joy from seeing others apply God's Word.

THE GIFT OF LEADING

The Speaking Gifts   **DAY FOUR**

The last gift we will look at from Paul's list in Romans 12 is the gift of **leading.** Closely akin to "administrations" in 1 Corinthians 12, the Greek word translated "leading" in Romans 12:8 literally means "stand in front of." **Administration** often involves guiding behind the scenes, while the gift of **leadership** requires standing out front, being highly visible. Administration seems aimed at tasks, but leadership is aimed at people. The gift of leadership is the ability to take charge and see that the job gets done. This person is good at dividing a task up between people and following through to make sure they do what is needed. If a task is delegated to one with the gift of leadership, it gets done. It is important to recognize and acknowledge that not everyone who fills a leadership position in a church will have the spiritual gift of leading. Some, however, are uniquely gifted to be effective as leaders.

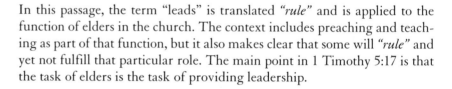 What instruction does Paul give in Romans 12:8 to those with the gift of leadership?

_____

_____

_____

_____

Paul tells those gifted as leaders that they are to exercise their responsibilities *"with diligence."* Leadership is one of the greatest needs in the body. When this gift is present and is applied diligently, others become more effective. Leaders in the body of Christ are able to recognize the resources around them and put them to use. It is the diligence of leaders, more than any other gift, which insures the proper working of the body.

In 1 Timothy 5:17, the word *"rule"* comes from the same Greek word as the word translated *"leads"* in Romans 12:8 (*proistemi*). Look at this passage and record your observations about what it says concerning the gift of leading.

_____

_____

_____

_____

Word Study
THE ROLE OF LEADING

The Greek word translated "to lead," in several passages of Scripture is *proistemi*, which comes from *pros*, "before or over," and *histemi*, "to stand." It means "to be over, to preside, to rule," and by implication means "to care for something diligently." Jesus made it clear that in the kingdom of God, this is a servant role, not a privileged position.

In this passage, the term "leads" is translated *"rule"* and is applied to the function of elders in the church. The context includes preaching and teaching as part of that function, but it also makes clear that some will *"rule"* and yet not fulfill that particular role. The main point in 1 Timothy 5:17 is that the task of elders is the task of providing leadership.

In 1 Thessalonians 5:12, the phrase *"have charge over"* is the same in the Greek as *"leads"* in Romans 12:8. What do you learn from this verse about leading?

_____

_____

_____

It is clear from the translation *"have charge over"* that leading involves being responsible for others. We also see that leading includes diligent labor *"among you."* A leader cannot be effective without relationships and involvement in the lives of those being led. To be withdrawn from people is to lead ineffectively. We also see here that leading involves giving instruction or admonition.

Read 1 Timothy 3:1–5, 12. The word *"manages"* in verse 4 is translated from the same Greek word we have been studying (*proistemi*). Make note of what you glean from this passage.

_____

_____

_____

First Timothy 3 identifies the character qualities of one who would be an elder or a deacon. Aside from the clear indications that these positions should only be filled by men, we are also told that men who aspire to these positions must manage their own households well. While this passage ultimately points to church leadership, it makes clear that this is not the only arena where the leading gift functions. One who is a good leader at home will also be a good leader elsewhere. The use of the word "manage" in translation paints a picture of the guiding and delegating work of a leader.

In the New Testament, perhaps the clearest picture we have of someone with the gift of leadership is the apostle James, the brother of Jesus. He was the recognized leader among all the leaders of the mother church in Jerusalem. In Acts 15, in a meeting with such prominent leaders of the first century as Paul, Barnabas, and Peter, it is James who is clearly in charge. This does not mean that he is more important than the rest, but rather that he serves a unique role of blending together the gifts and talents of this diverse group in such a way that all are more effective and the body is benefited. This is leadership in action.

FOR ME TO FOLLOW GOD

The Speaking Gifts **DAY FOUR**

Second Timothy 3:16–17 reminds us that the tool of the trade for the speaking or equipping gifts is God's Word. It says, *"All Scripture is inspired by God and profitable for teaching, for reproof, for correction, for training in righteousness; so that the man of God may be adequate, equipped for every good work."* The result of properly handling God's Word is that others are equipped. Some have seen a reflection of the four equipping gifts in this passage, as the verses mention the different ways Scripture works. According to this interpretation, the mention of teaching obviously correlates to the gift of teaching; *"reproof"* is a natural function of the gift of prophecy; *"correction"* relates to the exhorter; and *"training in righteousness"* is viewed as the role of the leader. While such a conclusion cannot be held with certainty, we do know that the result of the proper use of God's Word is that God's people are *"equipped for every good work"* (Ephesians 4:11–12).

This theory is useful in drawing some distinctions in the subtle differences between the speaking gifts. Teachers focus on the mind and the understanding. They show us what to believe. Prophets focus on the will. They confront us with how we stray from God's desires and design. Exhorters help us to get back on track and minister to our motivation. The gift of exhortation, more than any other gift, puts a spotlight on application. Leaders guide the entire process toward its intended end: righteousness. God has given each of the four speaking gifts to the body so that the gospel message is properly proclaimed. Again, one gift is not more valuable than the other. All gifts are a necessary part of God's plan for His people.

 How does this lesson apply if I do not have a speaking gift?

If you don't have a speaking gift, you may think this lesson has little for you in the way of practical application, but that conclusion would be wrong. Each of us needs what those with speaking gifts have to offer. Consider the following different needs listed and identify where you might look for help in those areas.

If you have a doctrinal question, the best person to seek out would be one with the gift of teaching. Who are some teachers you know?

_____

_____

_____

_____

If you are struggling with sin in any area, the gift of prophecy can be especially helpful. Whom do you know with the gift of prophecy?

_____

_____

If you need further training in living the Christian life or in being effective in ministry, exhortation is usually the right gift to seek out. Who are some exhorters you know?

_____

_____

If you need guidance, discernment in where to serve, reconciliation with a brother, or life direction, those gifted as leaders will be helpful. Whom do you know with the gift of leading, based on what you learned in this lesson?

_____

_____

APPLY How does this lesson apply if I do have a speaking gift?

If God has endowed you with one of the speaking or equipping gifts, then it is important for you to discern which one you have. One of the problems I've observed in leadership is that many assume that if they have a speaking gift, they have the gift of teaching. That is not always the case. It is important to distinguish between these gifts in order to know your own strengths as well as what you need from others. The following questions/statements are helpful in distinguishing between the speaking gifts. Perhaps some of these statements apply to you.

❏ If teachers were given the choice between research and presenting a lesson, they would most likely choose research.

❏ For teachers, research is not just a means to prepare a message, but a method of answering questions in their own minds.

❏ Teachers evaluate worship by how it measures to a scriptural pattern rather than by the atmosphere.

❏ Teaching gifts come with great motivation to study for long periods.

❏ Exhorters like to follow up with people to encourage growth.

❏ Those with the gift of exhortation are naturally gifted in illustrations.

❏ Exhorters are passionate that application take place.

❏ Exhorters like their interaction with the audience as much as with the material.

❏ Having the gift of prophecy is being able to discern what is wrong with a church or an individual.

Each of us needs what those with speaking gifts have to offer.

- ☐ Those with the gift of prophecy are not shy about confronting what is wrong.

- ☐ Prophets are more concerned with how the Lord feels about a situation than with how any person feels.

- ☐ Leaders are able to see unused resources and bring them to bear on needs in the body.

- ☐ Leadership gifts come with a passion that projects and tasks are completed.

- ☐ Leaders are motivated more by solutions than by processes.

- ☐ Those with the gift of leadership delight in seeing the organization run more smoothly.

These statements are not exhaustive but may be helpful in distinguishing between the speaking gifts.

 As you can see from the last two lessons, God has made each of us unique to be of use to others. We will never be satisfied or complete living only for ourselves. He has made us ministers. Close out this week's lesson with a prayer of thankfulness for how the Lord has made you and others around you.

_____

_____

_____

_____

_____

_____

_____

_____

_____

_____

_____

_____

_____

_____

_____

Identifying Your Service Gift

The year was 1940. The French army had just collapsed under the assault of Hitler's *blitzkrieg* or "lightning war." Earlier, the Dutch had been overwhelmed along with the Belgians. The British army, trapped in France, broke free and retreated to a tiny fishing town on the coast—the French channel port of Dunkirk. To their front faced the might of Hitler's Third Reich, and to their backs, the open sea. In the words of Churchill biographer, William Manchester, "It was England's greatest crisis since the Norman conquest," and because the United States had not yet entered the war, England was forced to defend its homeland alone. Yet it hardly stood a chance with more than three hundred thousand of its finest young men trapped on the other side of the English Channel—doomed to die. Any rescue attempt seemed feeble and futile in the time remaining. The Fuhrer's troops were only miles away. British commanders told King George VI that they would be lucky to save seventeen thousand troops—less than ten percent of the men. The House of Commons was warned to prepare for "hard and heavy tidings." Politicians were paralyzed, the King was powerless, and the Americans could only watch from a distance. Then, just as doom for the British army seemed imminent, a strange fleet appeared on the horizon of the English Channel: It was perhaps the wildest assortment of boats ever

Primarily, paid professionals have always carried the heaviest workload in God's ministry. Of course, this is not His ideal design.

assembled in history. Trawlers and tugs, scows and fishing sloops, lifeboats and pleasure craft, smacks and coasters, sailboats, and just about any other type of vessel that was remotely seaworthy came to the rescue. Civilian volunteers manned each ship—English fathers sailing to rescue Britain's exhausted, bleeding sons. Manchester writes in the first volume of his epic biography of Winston Churchill, *The Last Lion*, that what happened in less than twenty-four hours in 1940 seems like a miracle even today—not only were all of the British soldiers rescued, but numerous other Allied troops were also saved. More than 338,000 soldiers were ferried across the channel that day. Those soldiers lived to fight another day and were instrumental in the eventual Allied victory.

The parallel in the Church today is striking. Paid professionals (ministers, missionaries, and full-time Christian workers) have most heavily carried the load of God's work in ministry, but that is certainly not God's design. The needs of the world are too great to be met by so few. Even the needs of one church are too great to be effectively met by the paid professionals. Everyone's efforts are needed if the Lord's work is to be done. Each of us must make a contribution, not just financially, but by offering our own gifts and service. That's the only way God's will is going to be done on earth. A church whose only worker is the pastor will be a church doing very little for the kingdom. God's design is for pastors to equip laymen so **they** can do the work of service.

But there is a problem. Today, the vast majority of Christians does not have any kind of personal ministry, and most have no idea what their spiritual gifts are. Even more startling is the reality that a great many Christians don't see any problem with the current state of affairs. They think ministry is for the elite—the special people of the kingdom. They think they are supposed to be spectators. But if that were true, why did God give each one of us a spiritual gift? Why does Scripture instruct us to employ that gift for the common good? Sadly, many think they have a spiritual gift for their own personal use and edification, but that clearly contradicts Scripture. Our gifts are to be used for the sake of others. God has made each Christian a minister! His work cannot be accomplished unless everyone participates.

DAY ONE

WHAT DO YOU WANT TO DO?

When we are walking closely with God, we want to do what He specifically enables us to do.

If we're all needed in the work of the kingdom, and if we're all able, how do we know where we fit? In this lesson, we will look at some key principles that will help you make your much-needed contribution to God's work. There are several steps in moving from spectator to server, and we'll explore them in future lessons, but first we need to find your fit. We'll do that by figuring out who you are. How has God gifted you? Moving from "pew warmer" to contributing servant requires that you know what your spiritual gift is—because it's not just what you do, it's part of who you are. Whenever you serve, you'll be using your spiritual gifts in your own special way, and knowing what those gifts are will help you avoid the frustration of serving in the wrong capacity or not serving at all.

Today we'll look at one principle you can use in identifying your spiritual gifts. It's wrapped in a simple question: What do you want to do? When you are walking closely with God, you'll want to do what He's specifically enabled you to do. **Personal Inclination**, when not driven by sin, is one of the clearest indicators of who we are. Fleshly desires—those motivated by pride or selfishness—cannot be trusted, but spirit-filled desires always point to God's will. You'll want to exercise your particular gift, and you'll be motivated to do so. Ministries relating to your gift (or gifts) will be your special concern. For example, a person with the gift of mercy will want to show mercy; a person with the gift of teaching will want to teach. Take some time to examine your desires.

📖 Take a look at Psalm 37:4 and answer the questions that follow.

What is the prerequisite to (gain?) the desires of our hearts?

_____

_____

Where do such desires originate?

_____

_____

The psalmist instructs us to *"delight"* ourselves in the Lord so that He will give us the desires of our heart. People interpret the last phrase of verse two quite differently. Some think that whatever we desire, we will get. Others believe that the desires of our heart come from the Lord when we delight to be close to Him. In some respects, I believe both interpretations are true. If we delight in God, He is molding the things we desire. He leads us to desire what He desires, and He is willing and able to fulfill those desires. Sometimes we have the idea (wrongly) that because we want something, it couldn't possibly be God's will. This kind of thinking is rooted in a distorted view of God.

📖 What does Psalm 145:19 say is needed for our desires to be realized?

_____

_____

We see in this psalm that the Lord *"will fulfill the desire of those who fear Him."* The word *"fear"* doesn't suggest that we should be afraid of Him, but rather that we should revere Him and fear displeasing Him. This idea seems to go hand in hand with Psalm 37:4. When we have a close relationship with God, our desires will reflect His, and He will be eager to fulfill them. That said, we should be vigilant to observe the desires we are drawn to when walking closely with God.

📖 Read through Exodus 2:11–15.

What do you think motivated Moses to kill the Egyptian?

_____

_____

_____

Was this the way God wanted to use him to deliver Israel?

_____

_____

I believe God has created our hearts to desire Him and a desire to follow His ways. We may not fully understand how those desires will be realized, but we do have an innate sense that He has placed within us. Moses was aware that God wanted to use him to deliver Israel from Egyptian bondage. I think that's what prompted him to kill the Egyptian soldier. He knew the end result; he just didn't yet know the means God would employ to accomplish it. It wasn't until he met God at the burning bush (Exodus 3) that the Lord revealed how He was going to make Moses a deliverer. Personal inclination points us in the right direction, but we must seek the Lord throughout the entire process to know His plan and His timing.

📖 Look at Galatians 5:17 and note how it applies to this principle of personal inclination.

_____

_____

_____

This verse presents a word of warning about reading too much into our desires. It must be a desire to do it God's way. It's possible that our desire is nothing more than a carnal wish for attention or the reward a gift brings. Some may want to rule, but they don't want to do it God's way. Such a desire isn't gift-oriented but greed-oriented.

Desire isn't the final test, but it is the first clue. It points us in the general direction of where we fit in God's kingdom and ministry. We need to be careful not to run ahead of God as we follow those desires, but at the same time, we should not dismiss them as irrelevant. Some good questions to ask are, "What do I enjoy doing for its own sake (not for rewards)? What are my special concerns?"

Word Study
DESIRE

The Greek word translated "desire" in Galatians 5:17 is *epithumeo,* from *epi,* "in," and *thumos,* "the mind." It means "to have the affections directed toward something, to lust, desire, long after." It is used of both healthy desires and sinful ones, such as coveteousness and lust.

Identifying Your Service Gift   DAY TWO

HOW DO OTHERS SEE YOU?

Personal inclination is one indicator of our spiritual giftedness, and we do want to be involved in the activities for which God has gifted us. But as we saw, desire can also mislead us. Because we are fallen creatures in a fallen world, not all our desires are from God. A second principle for discerning how (and where) God wants you to serve is **public recognition.** Not only will we desire the kinds of service for which we are gifted, but others will also recognize how God has made us. This second principle provides us a safeguard from being misled by desires that are not godly. Over time, as we say yes to the opportunities the Lord brings our way, others will see the Lord's blessing in areas where we are gifted. We can see this principle functioning in the body of Christ from the earliest days of the New Testament church.

The Church was born in the first century A.D. and experienced rapid growth. Three thousand believers were added to the Church on the day of Pentecost (see Acts 2:41). A short time later, Acts records five thousand men being added to the Church in one day (see Acts 4:4). Since only the number of men is mentioned, most scholars assume that whole households were converted, and the actual number could have been as many as twelve thousand.

Talk about church growth! But **numeric growth** has never been an end in and of itself for the Church. Jesus desires **spiritual growth** in the lives of those who become believers. The early church grew rapidly, and so did the needs and opportunities to serve.

📖 Look at Acts 6:1–7.

What need developed as the early church grew in size (verse 1)?

_____

_____

_____

How did church leaders handle this new need (verse 2)?

_____

_____

_____

Who selected leaders for this new ministry (verse 3)?

_____

_____

_____

What criteria were used to select these leaders (verse 3)?

_____

_____

_____

What were the results of engaging these new individuals in serving (verses 4, 7)?

_____

_____

_____

Perhaps you're already familiar with this passage, but we'll take a fresh look and see how it reveals rich principles about engaging in ministry. As the early church grew, so did its needs. If a congregation grows while the number of people serving in it stagnates, the ministry actually begins to shrink—needs go unmet, and adjustments must be made. But notice that even though the leaders of the first century church recognized the problem of widows being left out, **they** did not select the men themselves. They instructed **the congregation** to *"select from among"* them men they could put in charge of the task. For this to happen, the congregation had to recognize something in the lives of these men. First of all, they recognized their character. They were men of *"good reputation."* The congregation also saw the Spirit of God in them, and that they had wisdom. Regardless of our giftedness, these things must be present for us to serve effectively. As a result of having these men in charge of ministering to the practical needs of the congregation, the elders were able to devote their energies to *"prayer, and . . . the ministry of the word."* Because the deacons were serving and the elders were praying and equipping, *"the word of God kept on spreading; and the number of disciples continued to increase greatly in Jerusalem."*

Did You Know?

SEVEN SERVANTS

Seven men are mentioned in Acts 6 as being placed in charge of serving the "Hellenistic" (Greek) widows. It may be that the number "seven" was selected in keeping with the "seven of a city," which made up the local board of a Jewish community. All seven men have Greek, not Jewish, names. As such, they would feel more compassionate toward the Greek widows under their care.

Doctrine

THE MINISTRY OF DEACONS

While the seven of Acts 6 are not specifically called "deacons," traditionally they are viewed as such. This idea is supported by the use of the Greek word *diakonia* (translated "serve" in verse 1). It wasn't until later in the development of the church that "deacon" became an official office (see 1 Timothy 3), but clearly we see in this passage two levels of leadership, each with a different focus. The "twelve" elders of the congregation were focused on "prayer and the ministry of the word," while the seven were focused on meeting of practical needs. The former served by leading, while the latter led by serving.

While there are many important truths in this story from Acts 6, it's important to reiterate one essential detail about what was taking place. It was not the elders who selected men to serve the needs of the widows, but the congregation. As a result of the congregation's affirmation, these men were given a ministry. Their gifts and readiness to serve were affirmed by public recognition. Sometimes God makes others aware of our gifts.

📖 Read Acts 11:22–26. How did Paul get to Antioch, and why do you think he was brought in that way?

_____

_____

_____

As we saw in a previous lesson, the apostle Paul started his vocational ministry because Barnabas sought him out and invited him to join the work at Antioch. We know from 2 Timothy 1:11 that Paul was a gifted teacher. Obviously, Barnabas recognized this and knew Paul would be invaluable in Antioch. After Paul arrived there, we are told that for a year they *"taught considerable numbers."* Don't miss this one detail though—Paul was there because Barnabas saw he was needed and invited him. Barnabas recognized his giftedness and his readiness to serve.

> **You find your giftedness by serving, not by waiting.**

The Church will recognize your giftedness over time and make use of it. You will be given opportunities to minister. Where has God already used you in the body? Look for those areas where, over and over again, God has used you in a special way. If you are walking closely with God and serving in the right way, you don't have to drum up business. In the beginning though, you must realize that your opportunities to serve will most likely be very general at first and then become more specific as you prove yourself.

First Corinthians 12:7 says spiritual gifts are given *"for the common good."* When you exercise your giftedness, it will benefit the body; God will bless it and minister to others. A person with the gift of mercy will attract those who need mercy. Someone with the gift of helps will attract those with practical needs. But some say, "I haven't had any opportunities to serve, let alone a chance for God to bless it." Ask yourself these questions:

❑ Am I filled with the Spirit?
❑ Am I willing to serve where God opens a door?
❑ Am I waiting for a certain door to open out of fleshly desires?

Determine to say yes to the next opportunity God gives you. As you do that, He will refine and define your giftedness. This is a key principle—you find your giftedness by serving, not by waiting. What opportunities to serve has God placed before you and where has he blessed your service?

Identifying Your Service Gift

DAY THREE

WHAT HAS GOD REVEALED?

To be thorough, we need to address an unusual way in which God occasionally identifies our giftedness: **prophetic declaration**. This is definitely not the norm, but God sometimes speaks this way. I am reminded of an incident concerning my paternal grandfather. He was saved as a young man from a life of "moonshining" and drunkenness and later became a preacher. One day when I was very young, I was playing in my grandfather's backyard with all my cousins. On this occasion he leaned over to my father and singled me out from all the grandchildren saying, "Eddie will be the one who picks up where I leave off." Much like my grandfather, I was saved from a life of ill repute—a life of drugs and drug dealing. The year my grandfather died was the year I went into the ministry. Was it just the power of his suggestion that led me into the Lord's service? No. It wasn't until after I was in the ministry that my father shared the incident with me, and it was an affirmation that I was in the right place. Prophetic declaration is when God tells someone else before He tells us.

📖 Take note of what's written in 1 Timothy 1:18 (and the surrounding context) regarding prophecies and Timothy's spiritual giftedness.

_____

_____

_____

_____

_____

Here we see that prophecies had been previously made concerning Timothy. Not much specific detail is given in this verse, but if we look at the context of the chapter, it begins with references to Timothy's teaching and instructional ministry (verses 1:3, 5). Verse 18 contains Paul's challenges to Timothy (mostly consisting of properly handling the Word and giving leadership in the church), and these were "in accordance with" the prophecies given about him.

📖 Now look at 1 Timothy 4:13–16 and see what else you learn about these prophecies.

_____

_____

_____

_____

In this passage, the prophecies about Timothy become much clearer. Verse 14 tells us that his spiritual gift was bestowed upon him "through prophetic utterance." Apparently at his ordination, certain prophecies were made about his spiritual giftedness. (Notice the mention of laying on of hands by the presbytery or elders.) It is obvious from the instructions Paul gives in verses 13, 15, and 16 that Timothy had a teaching gift.

To understand Timothy's experience and how he got his gifts, it's necessary to take a look at verse 14 as it was originally written in Greek. The word "bestowed" is the key term. Is it saying that Timothy received his gifts through prophecies and laying on of hands? If so, then we should be practicing the same. But a key observation from the Greek makes the issue more clear. The term "bestowed" is in the passive voice in Greek. To quote _The New Linguistic and Exegetical Key to the Greek New Testament_ (Cleon L. Rogers Jr. & Cleon L. Rogers III, Grand Rapids: Zondervan Publishing House, 1998, p. 495), it is "theologically passive, indicating that God was the giver." It is not saying the elders "bestowed" his gift, for they had no power

The Greek word translated "confess" in the New Testament (*homologeo*) is derived from two words—*homo*, which means "the same," and *logeo*, which means "to speak." Literally, the word means "to speak the same thing" or "to agree."

to do so. Instead, the passive voice makes it clear that the bestowal came from God, and the elders only affirmed it and prophesied about Timothy's future ministry. Further, Rogers and Rogers add that the term "with" (Greek—*meta*) does not express that the laying on of hands was the means of bestowing Timothy's gift—it was merely accompaniment.

📖 Read through the account of Paul's conversion in Acts 9 and record what God revealed in to Ananias concerning Paul's future ministry (verses 15–16).

_____

_____

_____

_____

God revealed to Ananias what Paul's future ministry would be before He told Paul. God was calling Paul to minister to the Gentiles, and he would experience much suffering in this calling. As a result of this prophecy, Ananias called Paul *"brother."* Quite a change from Ananias' previous concerns regarding Paul's persecution of believers (verses 13–14)!

What can we apply in our own lives from these examples of prophetic declaration? Instead of struggling with the mechanics of how this happens, let's focus on what actually happened in each of these cases. God revealed to certain believers key aspects of another believer's gifts and future ministry. In Timothy's case, it's clear the information was revealed to people in leadership. Similarly, God may also choose leaders over us and reveal our gifts and ministry to them first. How God chooses to tell them doesn't necessarily have to be dramatic; it may just be that God gives them wisdom.

Identifying Your Service Gift

DAY FOUR

ONCE I KNOW IT, HOW DO I USE IT?

Much of our time has been spent focusing on identifying our spiritual gifts, but this is just the first step in moving toward participation in an active ministry. We should not only understand what our gifts are, but we should also be able to use them properly. A spiritual gift has its source in God, not ourselves; therefore, it ought to glorify God, not us. Just because something is spiritual or done in the name of Jesus doesn't mean that it's right. If our gift is used as God desires, there ought to be a **proper confession**. Our gifts should further God's work, and not that of any individual. There is only one kingdom to be built, and it is the kingdom of God.

📖 Just because something is supernatural doesn't mean that it is of God. Not all supernatural gifts come from the Holy Spirit. Identify what Matthew 7:22–23 says about this.

_____

_____

_____

_____

These verses form an amazing statement! Jesus tells us that on the day of judgment, many will say, " *'Did we not prophesy in Your name, and in Your name cast out demons, and in Your name perform many miracles?'"* And yet, the next verse makes it clear these are not believers. Jesus' verdict: *"I never knew you."* Again, just because something appears supernatural doesn't mean that it's of God.

📖 Look at 1 John 4:1–3 and write down what it says about testing the spirits.

_____

_____

_____

John makes an important point here—*"do not believe every spirit."* He warns us some are false prophets, and he even tells us how to recognize them. First, they will deny that Jesus Christ has come in the flesh. Second, they will not *"confess"* Jesus. The word "confess" means "to say the same thing," so they will not be saying the same thing about Jesus that Scripture does.

📖 What does 1 Corinthians 12:3 suggest about the problems in that church?

_____

_____

_____

_____

Corinth was not a healthy church. They lacked no gifts, but because of improper use, their gifts were not making them a mature and stable church. Apparently, while speaking in tongues, some were actually saying, "Jesus is accursed" instead of calling Him "Lord" as they should.

If a man is of God, he will always put Jesus Christ in His proper place—on the throne. Any movement, any ministry, any work that puts anything above Jesus is not in the will of God. He who is of God and is walking closely with God always puts Christ in His proper place—at the center of all things.

He who is of God and is walking closely with God always puts Christ in His proper place—at the center of all things.

FOR ME TO FOLLOW GOD

Identifying Your Service Gift **DAY FIVE**

Thus far, we've studied four important principles about identifying our spiritual gifts and properly putting them to use. We've seen the value of personal inclination and public recognition. We've looked at the uniqueness of prophetic declaration and the significance of proper confession. There is just one more method that may be helpful in identifying your spiritual gifts: **prescriptive testing.** Many people over the years have identified their gifts using a spiritual gifts test. There are quite a few such tests available from many different sources. Each has its own strengths and weaknesses. In taking these kinds of tests, it's important to realize that they cannot give you a definitive answer. However, they can be beneficial in starting you off in the right direction. Ultimately, our gifts are defined and perfected in the context of actual ministry, and not in answering questionnaires. But such tests can save us time and frustration by giving us a good start.

Your church may have a particular spiritual gifts test for you to take. If not, I recommend the one used by Bill Gothard Ministries (Box 1, Oak Brook, Illinois, 60521). As you work through the test, be aware that some things could skew the process. Sometimes we don't answer from our heart, but based on what we think is the right answer. Any ministry or church has certain values—virtues that are prized and emphasized. Over time, indoctrination can leave us with rote answers we perceive as correct, but which may or may not fit us personally. For example, if your church places a premium on evangelism, your answers may gravitate toward that, even if your personal strengths lie elsewhere. If you participate in a ministry that applauds in-depth Bible study, your answers could reflect a tendency for teaching, even if you don't have that gift. Because most ministries and churches don't value all gifts in a balanced way, it's possible you may also see certain gifts as more significant than others, and you will tend to affirm those things even if they are not your own personal endowment. In order to get the most out of any prescriptive testing, you must answer questions honestly by focusing on your own passions and experiences.

 What are some biases your church or ministry holds that might affect the outcome of your testing?

_____

_____

_____

_____

Another influencing bias factor in prescriptive testing is the lack of a personal involvement in ministry. If you have not been involved, or have spent very little time, in the life of a church or ministry, your answers will reflect that. It's okay though—don't be discouraged. Your goal is in the future, not the past, and since your gifts are part of who you are, they will be apparent in life and not just in church. They will be expressed at work, in your neighborhood, and in your home. However, since most test questions focus on church-based ministry experiences, you do need to be aware of your service record there and allow for it if the results are not conclusive or clear.

 Do you feel your involvement in ministry will accurately reflect who you are?

_____

_____

Maturity, ironically enough, is yet another factor that can affect your test results. As we "grow up" spiritually, we become more Christ-like, and we develop strengths in other areas as well. Have you ever considered the fact that Jesus has (had?) all the gifts? Along the road to spiritual maturity, we'll see changes in ourselves that reflect Christ's character, even though we may not see them now. We'll become more merciful, giving and serving willingly, learning new truths and gaining wisdom to share with others following behind us. We may not have these certain gifts initially, but as we mature they will become apparent.

If you've previously taken a spiritual gifts test and didn't have clear results, your own spiritual maturity might be clouding the outcome. If you think this is the case, the following questions could help you interpret the results.

Principle #1: We are energized by our passions.
We tend to be energized when exercising our spiritual gifts, not drained. For example, if you are gifted as a teacher, you probably get pumped up, more energized, and excited when you begin to teach.

What areas consistently have such an energizing effect on you?

_____

_____

_____

_____

Principle #2: We are drained when serving outside our specific giftedness.
Even though we may develop other skills as we grow and mature, we will lose energy and stay drained if we are not primarily serving with the spiritual gifts specifically given to us. For instance, I've learned administrative abilities over the years serving in various ministry capacities, but when I spend hours serving in this way, I find myself drained in a way that doesn't happen when I am studying and teaching.

What types of service tend to drain you even though you can do them effectively?

_____

_____

_____

_____

_____

Principle #3: God affirms our service in the area of our specific giftedness.
God's blessing will be on us when we serve in our area of specific giftedness. Better results (or the most fruit) occur when serving this way. For example, if you have the gift of teaching, you will bear much fruit when you teach. Life-altering changes will begin to happen through your ministry.

Where do you sense affirmation from God and others when you serve?

_____

_____

_____

_____

_____

_____

Principle #4: Our giftedness opens doors for the gospel.
Since we are called to share Christ with others, God will use our gifts as stepping stones to spread the gospel. Our gifts are the keys that unlock doors for the gospel. For those with the gift of service, helping out a neighbor with practical needs might make him receptive to your faith. If mercy is your gift, then showing mercy to someone may open the door and lead to other opportunities to discuss the Lord.

Doctrine
PRINCIPLES OF GIFTEDNESS

- Serving in our giftedness energizes us.
- Serving outside our giftedness drains us.
- God affirms service in our giftedness.
- Our giftedness opens doors for the gospel.

What seems to bring you the most opportunities to talk to others about spiritual matters?

_____

_____

_____

_____

As you reflect on any spiritual gifts test you have access to along with the questions above, what do you find are your spiritual gifts?

_____

_____

_____

_____

APPLY After completing the projects thus far, I believe my spiritual gifts are:

PRIMARY GIFT:

_____

SECONDARY GIFTS:

_____

_____

_____

_____

Take a moment to write out a prayer to the Lord. Ask Him to confirm your specific gifts and thank Him for how He's made you.

_____

_____

_____

_____

_____

_____

_____

_____

_____

_____

_____

_____

_____

_____

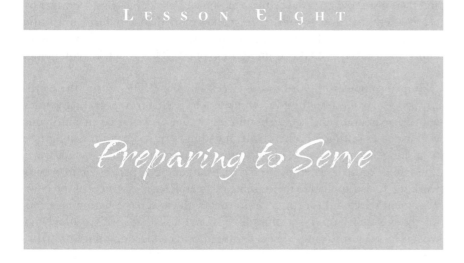

Preparing to Serve

How does one become an accountant? I've never spent much time thinking about that because it doesn't interest me. The accounting gene is missing from my DNA makeup. But one of my sons would make a great accountant. He likes numbers and he manages them well. Should he decide to become an accountant, though, he'll have to go to college and study hard. He'll have to develop certain skills and demonstrate his mastery of them. Then he'll have to graduate, and move on to take, and hopefully pass, the CPA exams. Only when he's successfully completed all these steps can he become a certified public accountant. Not surprisingly, similar steps are required to succeed in most professions. Becoming a lawyer takes college and law school. An aspiring physician goes through years of college, more years of medical school, and finally even more years of medical residency. In addition to all that, he must also attend extra training required for his specialization. But it isn't only professional jobs that require training. Labor-intensive jobs require skilled training as well. An electrician must first be an apprentice. Hanging on the walls of my auto mechanic's shop is framed evidence of his certification to perform various specialized tasks in his field. Even when my daughter got a summer job as a lifeguard, she still had to have specific training.

What does it take to be equipped to serve God?

What does it take to be equipped to serve God though? There once was a time in the Church when all a young man had to do was come down to the altar at the invitation to "surrender to preach" and in a week or two he might be preaching from the pulpit. A Sunday school teacher might be nominated by a committee because of faithful attendance and giving, even if he or she had never taught the Bible. And of course, everyone is qualified to work in the nursery, right? But is that really all there is to ministry? Do we say yes to God and then just show up? Maybe that's all some of us do, but if so, we won't be nearly as effective as we could be. As it takes more than a uniform and a rifle to make a soldier, so does it take more than just an altar call or invitation to minister effectively—it takes training, or to put it biblically, it takes equipping.

"Equip" is a powerful word in the Greek language. The root of the word, *artizo*, doesn't appear in the New Testament by itself, but appears many times with various prefixes. In Greek culture, the word was used in numerous ways, such as setting a broken bone, mending a frayed or torn fishing net, furnishing an empty house, or outfitting a ship for travel. The Greek word translated "equip" sometimes referred to attaining a perfect fit in woodworking. It also applied to the training of an athlete. The writers of the New Testament selected this expression to convey the idea of preparing believers for the work of God. It's a multidimensional task that involves supplying what is lacking, repairing what is damaged, and connecting things properly. All of this must take place if we, as sinful, fallen people, are to be transformed into servants in God's kingdom. This week, we'll look at the process of equipping and learn what must happen for a believer to prepare for service.

Preparing to Serve

DAY ONE

EQUIPPING INVOLVES TRUTH

Information is critical to training of any kind, and the Word of God is the wellspring of information used to equip servants for ministry throughout the ages. The Bible alone stands unequivocally as the most unique book in history. It was written over a period of thousands of years by some forty different authors from all walks of life: kings and shepherds, fishermen and farmers, even a tax collector and a physician. And yet the theme is incredibly consistent throughout all sixty-six books. How could men from different times, different places, different cultures, and different walks of life weave together such sublime words of wisdom? Peter explains: *"But know this first of all, that no prophecy of Scripture is a matter of one's own interpretation, for no prophecy was ever made by an act of human will, but men moved by the Holy Spirit spoke from God"* (2 Peter 1:20–21). Although He used many different people, God is the author of the Bible. It is His work and His words.

It's amazing to contemplate God as author, yet it demonstrates one more way in which He has accommodated His creation by revealing Himself in a way we could understand. John Wesley, founder of the Methodist Church, wrote: "I am a creature of a day, passing through life as an arrow through the air. I am a spirit coming from God and returning to God, hovering over the great gulf. A few months hence I am no more seen. I drop into an unchangeable eternity. I want to know one thing—if God Himself has condescended to teach the way. He hath written it down in a book. . . . Oh, give me that book! At any price, give me the book of God!" (from the preface to Wesley's book, *Standard Sermons,* 1746)

📖 Read 2 Timothy 3:16–17 and answer the following questions.

What does this passage say is the source of Scripture (verse 16a)?

_____

_____

For what is Scripture used (verse 16)?

_____

_____

_____

What is the intended result of applying Scripture in our lives (verse 17)?

_____

_____

_____

All Scripture is inspired by God—it is literally "God breathed." This is a powerful book we hold in our hands, and its application is very broad. It is profitable (or useful) for teaching—it tells us what to believe. It is profitable for reproof—it tells us what is wrong in our lives. It is profitable for correction—it tells us how to take what is wrong and make it right. It is profitable for training in righteousness—it builds honorable habits into our lives. But this work of Scripture is not merely for our own benefit. Its intended application in our lives is that we might be *"adequate"* and *"equipped"* for every good work.

Think about the message of this verse. The Word must come before the work. It's impossible for us to be equipped for good works apart from studying and applying the Word of God. Secular business training will not make a spiritual leader out of us. The world's methods will not make a minister. It takes truth to equip us—the Word of God. We must study the Scriptures to be equipped, but study alone is not enough.

📖 Look at 1 Thessalonians 2:13.

What does this verse say Scripture can do in us?

_____

_____

What is our part in the process?

_____

_____

_____

Paul wrote the Thessalonians and thanked them for acknowledging Scripture's power. They recognized that Paul's teaching was not just the impotent words of man, but the empowered words of God. Notice what Paul says the Bible can do. He speaks of the Word as that *"which also performs its work in you."* But we also have a responsibility in this process—we must **accept** God's Word as authoritative, and we must **believe**. Faith energizes Scripture's job of equipping in our lives.

D. L. Moody said, "I prayed for faith and thought that some day faith would come down and strike me like lightning. But faith did not seem to come. One day I read in the tenth chapter of Romans, 'Now faith comes by hearing, and hearing by the Word of God.' I had closed my Bible and prayed for faith. I now opened my Bible and began to study and faith has been growing ever since."

"One day I read in the tenth chapter of Romans, 'Now faith comes by hearing, and hearing by the Word of God.' I had closed my Bible and prayed for faith. I now opened my Bible and began to study, and faith has been growing ever since."

—D. L. Moody

The Word of God is able to fit us for God's service, but the goal of equipping is not merely our work. It is also for our walk. For without a walk with God our work for God is of no consequence.

📖 Look at 1 Peter 2:2 and 2 Peter 1:3–4 and write what you learn there about the role of Scripture in making us fit for the Lord's service.

_____

_____

_____

_____

_____

In 1 Peter 2:2 we are exhorted to long for God's Word as a newborn babe longs for milk. Such a pursuit allows us to grow with respect to our salvation. In 2 Peter 1:3–4 we see that God has *"granted . . . us everything pertaining to life* **and** *godliness, through the true knowledge of Him."* God's promises in His Word are *"precious and magnificent"* and through them we *"may become partakers of (His) divine nature."* We can become like Him—equipped for every good work.

What does it take to be equipped to serve? It takes the application of the Word of God in our lives so that we *"may be adequate, equipped for every good work."*

EQUIPPING INVOLVES TEACHERS

Each of us can look back on our education and remember classes we took and subjects we studied that made no visible difference in our lives. I used to joke that the only people who actually used algebra as adults are algebra teachers, although I'm sure this is an exaggeration. But many of us can also look back on school and identify a handful of teachers that made lasting marks on our lives. They inspired us and motivated us to learn, and in those moments, truth was imparted that helped shape us and make us who we are today. I recall teachers who captured my interest and who were lovingly honest about things I needed to work on. I'll never forget one conversation with Leona Saidak, my high school guidance counselor. After I scored well on the ACT college entrance exam, she challenged, "Why didn't you apply yourself more in high school?" She was right. I had graduated with a flat "C" average, majoring in woodworking. I was bright but bored and gave little effort in high school. I remember Nancy Majors, my high school English teacher, who wrote in my senior yearbook, "First of all, I hope your 47 unexcused absences in my class don't keep you from graduating, and second, I hope you live up to your great potential." Because I knew these ladies truly cared about me, their words were a real help. I think of Dr. Paul Walwick, my college advisor, who helped me discover my passion for communication and guided me to graduate with honors as the "Outstanding Student" from his department.

As I reflect on my education, I realize I learned quite a lot from following my own interests. But more importantly, God placed people in my life that had a hand in creating the person I am now. The same is true of equipping people to serve. Experienced men and women of God play an invaluable role in teaching and equipping us to serve.

📖 Read Ephesians 4:11–12 and answer the following questions.

Which of the main categories of gifts (speaking, serving, and sign) is reflected in the church leadership positions of verse 11?

_____

_____

What results when these gifted individuals minister?

_____

_____

_____

_____

What does that mean to us as we prepare to serve?

_____

_____

_____

_____

Doctrine

📖 **EQUIPPERS**

While clearly, the list we find in Ephesians 4:11 is in the context of spiritual gifts and is related to them, it is important to recognize that these are also leadership positions or offices. These gifted people are given to the church to equip all of us. While one would expect each of these to be related to the speaking gifts, they may also be seen as ministries given to the gifted. A pastor, for example, might have the gift of teaching, or he might have the gift of exhortation, leadership, or prophecy.

Traditionally, these leadership positions are filled by individuals with speaking or "equipping" gifts. Although positions within the church are emphasized here more than spiritual gifts, we do see two speaking gifts mentioned: prophecy and teaching. Individuals with these gifts are to work toward *"equipping . . . the saints for the work of service, to the building up of the body of Christ"* (Ephesians 4:12). In other words, their ministry is to outfit and prepare the rest of us for our ministries. Preparing to serve requires study of God's Word, but it also takes gifted individuals to teach us and train us—not just by telling us **what** to do, but by telling us **why,** showing us **how,** doing it **with** us, and building us **up** so that ultimately we are able to do it ourselves.

Equipping someone to serve takes more than just nominating him, patting him on the back, and sending him on his way. It takes specific training, godly role modeling, and encouraging feedback.

📖 Look at Mark 3:13–14 and identify how Jesus prepared the twelve for ministry.

_____

_____

_____

When Jesus selected His twelve disciples, His final goal was to train and equip leaders who could continue His ministry when He was gone. His strategy was not just to tell them what to do, but through relationship, teach them step by step how to minister. His call to them was first to *"be with Him,"* and then He would *"send them out."*

Jesus' earthly ministry with the Twelve had four distinct phases that correspond to the four main challenges He gave to His followers:

- "Come and See" (the observation phase)
- "Follow Me" (the apprenticeship phase)
- "Take Up Your Cross" (the enlistment phase)
- "Abide in Me" (the deployment phase)

What did it mean for the disciples to "*be with Him*"? Jesus' earthly ministry had four distinct phases, identifiable in the four different invitations He gave them. He began by telling them to "'*come and . . . see*'" (John 1:39). He didn't burden the process with heavy expectations. He merely invited them into His life to observe. This phase lasted about four months and probably included many more than just the twelve. It wasn't until later that He challenged His handpicked group to "'*Follow Me*'" (Matthew 4:19). The second phase required a greater commitment, as the disciples left their jobs to pursue more intense training. But that was not all the Lord had in mind. After this phase ended, He began to reveal His true purpose and spoke of the cross. He challenged each of His men to "*Take up his cross*" (Matthew 16:24), by making a permanent commitment to give up everything, including their own lives, to follow Him. This phase of Jesus' ministry was the most intense before the cross. But there was yet a fourth phase and is perhaps the easiest to overlook. It was His last invitation on the night of His arrest. He said to the remaining eleven faithful disciples, "'*Abide in Me*'" (John 15:4), and then He left them. He ushered in a phase of ministry in which He would no longer be physically present. This meant the disciples were required to carry the weight of responsibility. He was still committed to them and involved in their lives, but they did not have the luxury of His daily presence to lean on.

As you can easily see from the example of Jesus and the disciples, the process of equipping us to serve requires people in our lives who can train us, model for us what effective ministry looks like, and give us feedback as we progress.

📖 Examine 2 Timothy 2:1–2, and write what you learn about Paul's strategy for equipping people.

_____

_____

_____

_____

The apostle Paul exhorts Timothy, "And the things which you have heard from me in the presence of many witnesses, these entrust to faithful men, who will be able to teach others also." In this statement, we see reflected four generations of disciples with four different levels of maturity and ministry.

Paul had invested years of ministry in Timothy, who was now the "senior pastor," so to speak, at the church in Ephesus. Paul wrote 2 Timothy as he neared the end of his life. This book is often referred to as a "Pastoral Epistle" due to the wealth of practical instruction it contains for those in church leadership. Paul lays out a clear schematic of church structure here. The entry level for a disciple is the level of **others;** "others" being those who desire to have a ministry in their lives. Most church members are at this level, and it's important to note that some will never move beyond this level. They differ from **faithful men,** in that a) they are unfaithful, and/or b) they are unable "to teach others." Some won't reach a teaching level simply because of unfaithfulness; while others, even though faithful, won't reach that level simply because they are not gifted to teach. They will certainly be true disciples, exhibiting an abiding walk with Christ, a heart for the Word, effective prayer, and the fruit of Christian character. They will have a practical ministry, and they may even function as leaders on the level of deacon, but their ministry will not primarily be in teaching others.

Scripturally, the primary distinction between elders and deacons is that elders are "able to teach" (1 Timothy 3:2). In 1 Peter 4:10–11, we see the main serving gifts divided into two categories: a) speaking gifts (prophecy, teaching, leading, and exhortation) and b) serving gifts (mercy, giving, and service). Speaking gifts will tend to dominate the higher levels of leadership in the church and in ministry. Some will exercise these gifts on a large scale, while others will be most effective teaching in a small group. The third level, "**Timothys,**" are those who function as equippers.

Ephesians 4:11–12 indicates that God gave apostles, prophets, evangelists, and pastor/teachers "for the equipping of the saints for the work of service." Again we see that giftedness is a primary consideration for those who reach this level of service. What separates a "Timothy" from a "faithful man" is that a Timothy's focus is no longer simply ministering **to** people, but rather, ministering **through** people. His job is to equip others for effective ministry. Those on the fourth level are the **"Pauls,"** those who function as elders. "Pauls" are those with the giftedness, maturity, and ministry experience to impart vision and direction. They function as generals in the church, marshaling the troops to more effective service. A healthy, mature church will exhibit clearly all four levels of maturity and ministry function.

Regardless of our maturity level, we can always benefit from the input of godly and gifted mentors. Their experience and wisdom will serve to keep us effective and equipped. This process is greatly threatened when we stop learning and fail to heed the exhortation of those who've gone before us. God's Word equips us, but He also uses the ministry of gifted mentors.

> *"The things which you have heard from me in the presence of many witnesses, entrust these to faithful men who will be able to teach others also."*
>
> **2 Timothy 2:2**

EQUIPPING INVOLVES TRUST

Preparing to Serve **DAY THREE**

Let's consider what we've learned so far about being equipped. In Day One, we saw that it involves God's Word, and a key passage of Scripture that mentions being equipped is 2 Timothy 3:17. Speaking of the role of Scripture, Paul writes, *"that the man of God may be adequate, equipped for every good work."* Equipping involves Scripture—the Word must come before the work. In Day Two, we saw that the Bible is not the only tool God uses in preparing us to serve; He also uses teachers—gifted individuals investing in our lives. Ephesians 4:11–12 is another key passage that uses the term "equip." It tells us that God gave leaders to the church for the *"equipping of the saints for the work of service, to the building up of the body of Christ."* There is one more key passage that uses the term "equip," and it confirms the other two. Today, we'll look at the preeminent role of the Lord in equipping, and see the part our trust plays in that.

📖 Read Hebrews 13:20–21 and identify what it teaches about us being equipped.

_____

_____

_____

_____

These verses near the end of Hebrews are actually a prayer of benediction, and this is important in interpreting its message. Plainly, in addition to using the Word and mentors, the Lord Himself equips us to serve. However, since this is a prayer, it also points out that we must **trust** the Lord to do this work.

We need to seek the Lord and ask Him to prepare us to serve. This keeps us focused on Him and brings balance to the process. If we focus solely on using Scripture to equip us to serve, we run the risk of merely gathering information. If we focus only on seeking mentors to guide us, we end up with merely receiving training. Trusting the Lord in the process brings it all into balance. Seeking the Lord as we study the Word moves it from seeking information to seeking revelation. Seeking the Lord as we allow others to train us helps to guard us from letting one individual shape us into his or her own image. We are called to be like Jesus, not to be like someone else. Often training without trust produces imbalance instead of balance.

Look at Ephesians 2:10 with these principles in mind and write down what stands out to you.

_____

_____

_____

When we look at Ephesians 2:10, keeping in mind this issue of trusting the Lord, several key terms stand out. First, we are reminded that we are *"His workmanship."* If salvation is not by works, but rather by grace through faith (Ephesians 2:8–9), do we believe serving is somehow different? Serving the Lord is not simply us working for Him, but us allowing Him to work through us. Second, we see in this passage that God has created us for *"good works."* Serving is what we were made for. Third, God has a specific plan for those works. Our good works were *"prepared beforehand"* with the goal that we would walk in God's plan for us. We must seek Him and find our place in His plan   not just doing good works, but doing God's works.

Take a look at Philippians 2:12–13 and record your thoughts.

_____

_____

_____

_____

Word Study

TO WILL AND TO WORK

Paul tells us here in Philippians that we are to *"work out [our] salvation with fear and trembling."* I would paraphrase this statement as "work it out with an eye on pleasing God." How do we do this? Paul emphasizes obedience. We must obey God's instructions, given in His Word, and we must obey what His Spirit prompts us to do. But again we see this element of trust— *"for it is God who is at work in you."* We are not our own workmanship. Paul tells us here that God works in us in two ways. First, He works in us *"to will,"* or "to desire." When we are trusting Him, we want to do what He wills for us. Second, He works in us *"to work for His good pleasure."* As we seek Him and trust Him, we are enabled to work in ways that please Him.

This passage brings balance to the issue. Serving the Lord does require effort. I do not want to suggest an entirely passive "Let go, and let God" atti- tude. We should actively seek the Lord's direction in serving, search the

Scriptures, and seek out mentors. But we must always bear in mind that we serve as He wills, not as we will.

EQUIPPING TAKES TIME

Growth is a process, not a point. In Mark, we see a clear analogy from nature: when a plant grows, it begins with the blade, then comes the head, then the mature grain. As Miles Stanford puts it in his classic book, *Principles of Spiritual Growth,* "For most of us it has been a long season of growth from the tiny green blade up to the 'full corn in the ear.' So many seek to settle for this stage: saved, with heaven assured—plus a pacifying measure of Christian respectability, at least in church circles." Clearly, that view of faith sees salvation as nothing more than "fire insurance"—we are saved from the fires of hell. But God desires to do more than rescue us from the penalty of sin. He wants to make us like Himself, and He is patiently working toward that goal. Paul captured it well when he wrote, *"Not that I have already obtained it, or have already become perfect, but I press on in order that I may lay hold of that for which also I was laid hold of by Christ Jesus"* (Philippians 3:12). The amazing thing is that Paul had been a Christian for twenty-five or thirty years when he wrote that! Today we will begin looking at the reality that becoming equipped to serve will take time.

📖 Read Jesus' words in Luke 6:40.

What is a disciple like when the job is finished?

_____

_____

_____

_____

What does it take to get there?

_____

_____

_____

_____

How long do you think it takes to be *"fully trained"* in anything?

_____

_____

_____

_____

Jesus said, *"Everyone, after he has been fully trained, will be like his teacher."* The model of ministry is the apprenticeship model. After enough time, training, and experience, we become like those who train us. But being *"fully trained"* obviously takes time. The more skill required for the task, the longer it takes to be trained in it. The term *"fully trained"* here is the same root Greek word that is translated "equipped" (*katartizo*) in the other passages we have looked at.

The word "equipped" speaks both of a process and of the completion of that process. It takes time to be equipped for anything. In 1 Thessalonians 3:10, the apostle Paul spoke of wanting to have more time with the Thessalonians so he could "*complete what* [was] *lacking in* [their] *faith*" Again, the Greek word for "equip" (*katartizo*) is used, here translated "*complete.*"

📖 Identify what Paul told Timothy to do with his giftedness in 1 Timothy 4:14 and 2 Timothy 1:6 (notice also the verses around each passage), and what you think that means.

_____

_____

_____

_____

_____

Paul's first letter to Timothy presents a significant warning. It is possible for a gift to lie dormant, unused. "*Do not neglect the spiritual gift within you,*" Paul exhorts. In 2 Timothy 1:6, a letter written near the end of Paul's life, he again admonishes Timothy to "*Kindle afresh the gift of God that is in you.*" The phrase, "*kindle afresh*" literally means "to fan the flames." It conveys the idea of blowing on hot coals until they burst into flame. Just as fanning the flames helps a fire to burn more brightly, time spent in training helps to our gifts more effectively.

📖 Read through 1 Timothy 3:1–13, the biblical qualifications for elders and deacons.

What restriction does verse 6 place on those who can be elders, and why?

_____

_____

_____

_____

What does verse 10 say must happen before someone can be a deacon?

_____

_____

_____

Paul warns Timothy that an elder must not be "*a new convert*"—a new believer. His reasoning is that a new convert too quickly placed in a position of leadership is likely to become conceited or proud. Just as pride was the devil's undoing, so too it can be ours if we are not mature enough for the position given to us. Maturity is more than just technical training; it means we have the wisdom to exercise our training appropriately. Likewise, deacons cannot be placed too quickly. "*Let these also first be tested,*" Paul writes. They are only to be allowed the title and position if they have proven themselves to be "*beyond reproach.*"

Did You Know?

CULTIVATING GIFTS

Like Paul, Timothy probably had the gift of teaching. Notice in 1 Timothy 4:13–16, the instructions Paul gives for Timothy to develop his giftedness. He instructs Timothy to. . . .

- give attention to public reading of Scripture
- give attention to exhortation
- give attention to teaching
- take pains with these things
- be absorbed in them
- let his progress be evident to all
- pay close attention to himself
- pay close attention to his teaching
- persevere in these things

You may be thinking, *That is all well and good, but I am never going to be an elder or deacon.* Regardless, the principles behind these limitations hold true in some way for any position of service. Time is needed to both prepare us and, equally important, to **prove** us. In my years of service in vocational ministry, I have often met people who are very skilled and gifted but are new to the Church or ministry organization. The temptation is always there to quickly give them responsibilities, because the harvest is always more plentiful than the workers. Yet it is God's will that they prove themselves faithful in small things before they are given greater responsibilities. The most gifted individuals still have to prove themselves faithful in a new place and should not expect otherwise. Sometimes, I have seen gifted teachers sitting on the sidelines because they couldn't immediately be given a significant teaching role for which they considered themselves qualified. The result was often that they ended up doing nothing. Because they were unwilling to prove themselves faithful in lesser service, they never earned the confidence of leadership to do what they might be able to do.

My advice to anyone is: if you aren't being offered the position of service you feel you deserve and are able to fill, start working toward it by saying yes to what is available to you. It takes time serving to be proven. Psalm 78:70–71 says that God chose David, *"from the sheepfolds; from the care of ewes with suckling lambs … to shepherd Jacob His people."* David had first shown himself faithful with a small flock, and then God gave him a big one.

📖 Look at Philippians 2:22 in its context and write what Paul says there about Timothy.

_____

_____

_____

_____

In speaking to the Philippians about his disciple, Timothy, Paul writes, *"you know of his proven worth."* Timothy had proven himself to Paul as well as to the Philippians. When Paul wrote 1 and 2 Timothy, his disciple was probably serving as the lead elder or pastor of the church at Ephesus. He never would have gotten the chance if he hadn't first proven himself in smaller ways.

When we speak of being equipped to serve, we must realize that part of what qualifies us to serve is the confidence of those in leadership. That only comes with time and being tested. There are no shortcuts. We must have time in the Word of God; we must have training from qualified mentors; and we must trust God to work in our lives if we are to be prepared to serve. But we also must allow that being adequately equipped and trusted with responsibility will take time.

> Paul wrote of Timothy, "you know of his proven worth." Timothy had proven himself to Paul as well as to the Philippians.

FOR ME TO FOLLOW GOD

Preparing to Serve **DAY FIVE**

When I look back over my years of serving the Lord, I have to honestly admit that I have never suffered from a lack of confidence in my ability, even when I really wasn't ready for what I thought

I was. But God in His sovereignty has not opened doors of service for me that I wasn't yet ready for. In 1 Corinthians 12:5 Paul wrote, *"There are varieties of ministries, and the same Lord."* While there are lots of different opportunities to serve, the door is always opened by the same person—the Lord. I think one of the most important messages to hear about this subject of spiritual gifts is that real ministry only happens when God opens the door. We can "bust a door down" and make ourselves busy. We may even be able to become the center of attention. But it won't be real ministry unless God is in it. All of our activity will end up as wood, hay, and stubble unless it is initiated and energized by God. It is the Lord of the harvest who sends out laborers into **His** harvest. If we want to fit into His plans, then we need to cooperate with His process of equipping us.

Psalm 37:3 says, *"Trust in the Lord, and do good; dwell in the land and cultivate faithfulness."* This verse comes immediately before the verse that says, *"Delight yourself in the Lord and He will give you the desires of your heart."* If our heart is set on serving in a particular place or a particular way, this is good advice. We need to do good where we are, trusting God to give us the opportunity we want in His own time. He knows what it will take for us to be ready.

As we seek to apply this week's lesson, it is important to recognize that it builds on our previous ones. Hopefully by now, you have some sense of what your own spiritual giftedness is. But do you know what Scripture has to say about that particular gift? Part of being equipped to serve is being informed on what God thinks about a particular kind of service. One of the ways you can find out such information is to do a topical or word study. For example, if your gift is mercy, then you might want to look that word up in *Nave's Topical Bible* to find Scriptures that address that subject. Or you could look the word up in a concordance and study every time it appears in Scripture. While this may seem like a lot of work, if the subject is our giftedness, it ought to be very interesting. Remember, 2 Timothy 3:17 tells us it is the Word of God that equips us for every good work.

APPLY If you do a word study, you will want to look at related words as well. For example, if your gift is teaching, you might want to study the words "teach," "teacher," "teaching," and "instruction." What are some words related to your gift?

_____

_____

APPLY Another area we looked at for equipping is the role of teachers and mentors. Can you think of some people who could mentor you in your area of giftedness or whom you could serve alongside as an apprentice?

_____

_____

Who might direct you to such an opportunity? Check the people with whom you feel a discussion would be profitable.

❏ Pastor   ❏ Friend
❏ Discipler   ❏ School instructor
❏ Sunday School teacher   ❏ Other_____

"Trust in the LORD and do good; Dwell in the land and cultivate faithfulness. "

Psalm 37:3

These individuals may be able to help you answer the next two questions as well. Remember, Ephesians 4:11–12 tells us it is the role of spiritual leaders to equip *"the saints for the work of service."*

 What are some training classes you are aware of that might further equip you for your area of giftedness?

_____

_____

_____

Are there any good books you can read to instruct you further in your area of giftedness?

_____

_____

 As we saw in Day Three, we must trust the Lord to equip us to be able to serve Him. Are there any barriers to your trusting Him in that area?

_____

_____

_____

_____

Remember what Hebrews 13:21 tells us. The same God who raised up Jesus from the dead is the One we are trusting to equip us to do His will and work in us *"that which is pleasing in His sight."*

Finally, equipping takes time. Check the boxes below that apply to your own situation.

❑ Time is needed to. . . .
❑ Train me further
❑ Gain experience with a mentor
❑ Study what Scripture has to say about my gifts
❑ Prove my faithfulness and abilities to those in leadership over me
❑ Other: _____

As you seek to trust the Lord and take action in these areas, commit them to Him in a written prayer in the space below.

_____

_____

_____

_____

_____

_____

_____

"Now the God of peace. . . . equip you in every good thing to do His will, working in us that which is pleasing in His sight, through Jesus Christ, to whom be the glory forever and ever. Amen."

Hebrews 13:20–21

Notes

Moving from Equipped to Engaged

Perhaps the greatest deficiency in so much of the material written on the subject of spiritual gifts is that it is incomplete. Simply knowing what the spiritual gifts are is insufficient; we must also discern how God has gifted each of us personally and specifically. However, even discernment of this nature does not take us far enough. We must fan the flames of our giftedness, developing the gifts we have. Again, as important as equipping is, it's not the end of the journey. So what is the journey, and where does it end? One of the dominant scriptural metaphors of the Christian life is that of the "walk." In Ephesians 4:1, Paul says, *"I . . . entreat you to walk in a manner worthy of the calling with which you have been called."* In Ephesians 4:17, he says that as believers we *"walk no longer just as the Gentiles walk, in the futility of their mind."* Ephesians 2:10 teaches that we were created for good works *"which God prepared beforehand, that we should walk in them."* Later, in Ephesians 5:15–16, Paul exhorts us to *"be careful how* [we] *walk, not as unwise men, but as wise, making the most of* [our] *time, because the days are evil."* But if the Christian life is a walk, where are we walking? If this time on earth is a journey, where does it begin and where is it going?

I think we'd all agree that the spiritual journey begins at salvation. As I see it, the next step in that journey is what some refer

> "What is engagement? Think of it as the transmission in your car. When it is engaged, the gears mesh and the car moves. But if it is in neutral, the gears spin—but you don't get anywhere."
>
> —George Barna
> *Growing True Disciples*
> © 2001, published by
> Waterbrook Press.

to as "spiritual formation"—building into our lives the traits we need to walk with God. We pack these necessities in our spiritual suitcase and take them with us on our journey: prayer, Bible study, personal devotions, faith in God, and they all must be in place before we can begin serving others. But these foundational basics are not just what we start with and then move on from; these are qualities we must live out every day of our Christian lives. Only when these disciplines have been incorporated into our lives, are we ready to move toward "engagement." Christian pollster George Barna says, "What is engagement? Think of it as the transmission in your car. When it is engaged, the gears mesh, and the car moves. But if it is in neutral, the gears spin—but you don't get anywhere. It is like that in most congregations." (*Growing True Disciples: New Strategies for Producing Genuine Followers of Christ,* Colorado Springs, 2001) Do you feel this way? It's as if you're spinning away in neutral, never having fully engaged your gears (your gifts), and getting nowhere fast.

Engagement is more than simply working for God. It is walking with God and letting Him work through us. Our spiritual gifts are a large part of what He wants to do through us. How do we map out our own personal course? Do we simply decide what we'd like to do and then ask God to bless it? Heaven forbid! Ours is not a job of deciding, but of discerning. We must discern how God has made us and with what spiritual gifts He has endowed us. We must discern the unique passions He's built into us that motivate and direct us to service, and we must discern which opportunities around us are from Him—those doors of service He's opening for us. As we wait for opportunities to serve with our own specific, unique, and individual gifts, we may have seasons of basic, general service as we learn. The ultimate destination of the Christian walk is to find our personal course, to identify the individual race we are to run, and to find where we fit.

In Acts 13:25, Luke refers to John the Baptist "*. . . completing his <u>course</u> . . .*" (Acts 13:25). Think about this for a moment. God planned a course of ministry and had a life purpose for John; it wasn't a course John picked, but one chosen for him before he was ever born (see Luke 1:15–17). John understood that he did not send himself, but that he was "*sent*" by God (John 1:6, 33). The apostle Paul was also a "*sent*" man (Acts 13:4). In Acts 20:24 he says, "*But I do not consider my life of any account as dear to myself, that I may finish my <u>course</u> and the ministry which I received from the Lord Jesus.*" He understood that God had a course planned for him, and it was quite different than the course he had planned out for himself as a Pharisee and persecutor of the church. But he followed God's plan for his life faithfully. At the end of his life, he could honestly say, "*I have fought the good fight, I have finished the <u>course</u>, I have kept the faith.*" Paul recognized and lived out God's purpose for his life. Do we have that same sense of purpose? We should. Ephesians 2:10 tells us that the good works we were created for were "*prepared beforehand*" by God for us to walk in. He has a *course* for us to walk as well (see Ephesians 2:2). But how do we discover God's course for our lives? How do we find where we fit? First, finding out where we fit is a process, not a point. Most of us won't receive our course all in one package, but will see it unfold little by little as we walk with God, following our innate desires and discerning which opportunities He's placed before us. Our course begins with "thirsting," desiring the calling that God has placed in our hearts. It is followed by "training," preparing to serve. Next comes "testing," serving under the leadership of others and receiving input, direction, and correction. Finally comes "entrusting"—that point when we receive, or are entrusted with, our personal ministry or life calling.

ENGAGEMENT BEGINS WITH THIRSTING

In Israel, there are two major bodies of water: the Sea of Galilee and the Dead Sea. In Jesus' day, the Sea of Galilee was a site of industry. Peter, John, Thomas, and several other disciples were professional fishermen before they followed Christ. In fact, Galilee still supports a thriving fishing industry today. The Dead Sea, on the other hand, doesn't support life at all. Its high salt content makes it barren and lifeless. They stand in stark contrast to each other, so it's amazing to realize both are fed by the same source. These two bodies of water are connected by the Jordan River. The Sea of Galilee receives its life-giving water from the streams flowing down the mountains to the North, and then transfers that same water to the South. Then the water flowing down from the South, passes through the Promised Land, and is finally deposited into the Dead Sea. Why are two bodies of water so different then, when they both receive the same water? The answer lies in how they use what they receive. The same water flows into both, but only one gives from what it's been given, whereas the other just receives. There is a definite spiritual principle for us in this brief bit of geography. Many Christians today are overfed and underused, and the fault is not wholly theirs. They receive, but the channels are not open to give out of what they receive. They may even be equipped, but they are not engaged.

There are many reasons for "Dead Sea" spirituality. Sometimes a limited structure in ministry affords opportunity to only a select few. Sometimes, due to a lack of information, people with specific callings are not connected with corresponding opportunities. Sometimes, it's simply because selfish church-goers don't understand or heed Jesus' words, " *'It is more blessed to give than to receive'* " (Acts 20:35). Whatever the reasons, this problem is rampant in the church today. Lives not engaged in the service God gifted and created them for are barren and empty. So how do we avoid a "Dead Sea" spirituality? How do we move from equipped to engaged? The first step is thirsting.

Thirsting includes our desire to serve in a particular way, but is also rooted in a desire to serve in any way. It begins with recognizing everyone has a place in the work of God. He wants every, single one of us to be involved in ministry. Recall the metaphor of the church as the "body of Christ." What member of your body would you not want to function? Because God wants us in ministry, He places in our hearts a desire for ministry—a thirst.

📖 Look at 1 Timothy 3:1. How does thirsting relate to being an elder?

_____

_____

_____

Sometimes when we desire something, especially something like leadership, we think we must be wrong. Yet here Paul tells Timothy that it is right and appropriate to aspire to the office of elder. Desire is where becoming an elder begins.

Some years ago, a man was nominated to be the elder over the youth ministry at our church. Everyone agreed that he met the biblical qualifications of character. He had a proven track record in the church and in his family. He had leadership skills and the respect of all who worked in that area of the church. Yet he lacked one crucial qualification that kept him from the

Map of Palestine showing Sea of Galilee, Jordan River and Dead Sea

"It is a trustworthy statement: if any man aspires to the office of overseer, it is a fine work he desires to do."

1 Timothy 3:1

office of elder; he did not desire it. Engaging in ministry begins with desire—it begins with thirsting.

How about you? Do you desire a particular ministry? If you do, it may be that God has placed that desire in your heart. If you don't, it may be because you've never seen yourself having a ministry at all. The beginning of a specific desire may start with a general desire to serve, motivated by biblical conviction. Perhaps you aren't convinced that everyone needs to have a ministry.

📖 Read Ephesians 4:16.

How is the whole body fitted and held together?

_____

_____

_____

What happens when each individual part works properly?

_____

_____

_____

Word Study

EACH INDIVIDUAL PART

In the King James Version, the word "every" appears twice in Ephesians 4:16, but in the Greek, two different words are used. When referring to "every" joint, the Greek word *pas* is used. It carries the idea of "the whole or a totality" and places the emphasis on all of us serving. When referring to "every" part, the Greek word *hekastos* is used. It carries the idea of "each one separately" and places the emphasis on our individual responsibility. The New American Standard Bible (NASB) translates this second "every" as "each individual part."

What will it take for the body of Christ to do God's work? Every one of us. The whole body is fitted and held together by each person's contribution. When each person works properly, the body grows and builds itself up in love. Being biblically convinced that ministry is meant for everyone is certainly a motivating factor in our desire to serve. That general desire, when developed, will then lead us to more specific desires that are more in keeping with our specific calling.

What does it take for this vision to become reality? Look at what Ephesians 4:17 says: "This I say therefore, and affirm together with the Lord, that you walk no longer just as the Gentiles also walk, in the futility of their mind." Futile living must be put aside so God's desire for His church can be realized. The selfishness of the old life must be put away, and we must learn to do that which truly matters. Titus 3:14 exhorts, "And let our people learn to engage in good deeds to meet pressing needs, that they may not be unfruitful." We must learn to live for eternal concerns instead of futile, temporal, fleeting matters. Only through living with an eternal mindset will we find the personal satisfaction and fulfillment we long for.

📖 Read John 4:34–37.

What did Jesus say was His food?

_____

_____

What do you think of when Jesus compares these things to food?

_____

_____

_____

_____

What do those who work in God's harvest fields get (verse 36)?

_____

_____

An interesting picture emerges when Jesus compares doing God's will and accomplishing His work to the food that nourishes us. Food accomplishes two objectives. First, it sustains our bodies since we cannot live without it. Second, it satisfies our hunger and is pleasurable to us as well. In the same way food affects our human bodies, serving the Lord sustains and satisfies our spiritual needs. Jesus says those who harvest in God's fields will reap the benefits of fruit for eternal life. Certainly this speaks of eternal reward, but beyond that there is the wage of a satisfied life.

When we seek fulfillment outside of God's design, we are never satisfied. Proverbs 14:14 tells us, *"The backslider in heart will have his fill of his own ways, But a good man will be satisfied with his."* We must desire a godly existence if we expect to live a fulfilling life. Ralph Barton, once one of America's foremost cartoonists, left this suicide note: "I have had few difficulties, many friends, great successes; I have gone from wife to wife and from house to house, visited great countries of the world, but I am fed up with inventing devices to fill up twenty-four hours of the day" (*The Total Man*, Dan Benson; Tyndale House Publishers, 1977, pp. 19–20). He'd climbed the ladder of worldly success only to discover it was leaning against the wrong wall.

Desire is the beginning of engagement, but only if we have learned to desire correctly. Psalm 37:4 tells us, *"Delight yourself in the LORD; And He will give you the desires of your heart."* If we delight in Him, He will give us godly desires and then fulfill those desires and satisfy our souls.

"I have had few difficulties, many friends, great successes; . . . but I am fed up with inventing devices to fill up twenty-four hours of the day"

—Ralph Barton's suicide note

ENGAGEMENT REQUIRES TRAINING

Moving from Equipped to Engaged **DAY TWO**

The first step in becoming engaged in ministry is thirsting. We must cultivate a desire to serve, and we must look at the desires for particular service that God gives us. If He is calling us to do a work, He will place a desire for it in our hearts. But desire alone is not enough. To engage in effective service, we must be trained and equipped. Last week, in the lesson on preparing to serve, we looked at this idea of becoming equipped. We saw that equipping is the result of four ingredients working together in our lives: the Scriptures, mentors, trusting God to work in our lives, and time. Today we will take these four items a step further and identify some specific areas where these four ingredients must be brought to bear in our lives.

📖 How does Paul instruct Timothy to develop his spiritual gift of teaching in 1 Timothy 4:13–16?

_____

_____

_____

_____

Paul challenges Timothy not to neglect the spiritual gift God has given him. Like Paul, Timothy had the gift of teaching. Notice the instruction Paul gives Timothy to develop his giftedness. He instructs Timothy to give attention to public reading of Scripture, and to exhortation and teaching. He charges him to *"take pains with these things"* and to *"be absorbed in them."* He wants Timothy's progress to be noticeable. Paul coaches him to *"pay close attention"* to himself and his teaching and to persevere.

All of us have spiritual gifts, but many of us don't develop them through training as Paul instructed Timothy to do. The first and most obvious area in preparing us to serve is in skill development. For example, someone wanting to become an effective teacher would definitely have to develop teaching skills. However, skills alone are not going to make one effective in ministry. There is much more to ministry than just learning your "tools of the trade," so to speak.

📖 Read 1 Timothy 1:5–6 and identify what must accompany Timothy's teaching skill.

_____

_____

_____

> *"Though I speak with the tongues of men and of angels, and have not charity, I am become as sounding brass, or a tinkling cymbal."*
>
> *1 Corinthians 13:1*

Paul makes clear to Timothy that teaching is more than just imparting information. The goal of instruction is love. In 1 Corinthians 13:1, after teaching on gifts, Paul says that speaking *"with the tongues of men and of angels"* without love is just making noise. In Ephesians 4:16, Paul speaks of the body being built up *"by that which every joint supplies."* What is a joint? It's not an individual part, but the place where two parts meet. Two bones can be perfectly healthy, without fractures or weaknesses, but if they become dislocated—pulled apart at the joint—they will not function properly. Ministry not only involves using our gifts; it requires building godly relationships.

Developing relationship skills is an essential part of training for any ministry. I know men and women with great gifts and high intellect who aren't effectively serving because they lack the necessary relational skills. Imparting what you know is important, but communicating it in a loving and godly manner is even more important. It is the key to get people listening to you. Thus, the second area of training to serve is in building relationship skills. But training doesn't stop there.

📖 Look at Mark 9:14–29.

Write down your observations regarding why the disciples couldn't cast out this demon.

_____

_____

_____

_____

What similarities do you see between that and training to serve?

_____

_____

_____

Mark 9 tells us the story of how the disciples failed in their service—in this instance, they could not cast out a demon inhabiting a young boy. The boy's father had asked them for help since Jesus was not available. They tried, and were unsuccessful. We see the first indication of why the disciples failed in Jesus' response in verse 19. Here He addresses the crowd (including the disciples) as an *"unbelieving generation.'"* This same idea is reiterated in verse 23 when He instructs, *"All things are possible to him who believes."* Apparently, the disciples don't understand His point, though, because later they asked Him privately why they'd failed. Jesus responds, *"This kind cannot come out by anything but prayer."* How does Jesus' statement relate to belief and unbelief? The disciples failed because they trusted themselves and their training instead of trusting God to do the work. One crucial component of training for ministry is learning to trust—not in ourselves and in our own abilities, but in God. It is He who does the work through us.

Training is the next step once we've determined how we are specifically gifted; however, nothing in this process can substitute for a genuine trust in God. A true servant of the Lord combines proper training and cultivating healthy relationships with an unwavering trust in God. We'll learn more about this in subsequent lessons, but for now it's helpful to be aware of these concepts.

ENGAGEMENT REQUIRES TESTING

For more than two decades I've served in Christian ministry, and I've witnessed many attempts at ministry and seen many mistakes made, most repeatedly with predictable consequences. One of the most common ways a church places people in service is by what I term the "warm body" approach. Often the task of finding people to serve in the local church is given to a nominating committee, whose job it is to then talk people into serving in some capacity they've never considered, didn't volunteer to do, and don't really want to do. The goal eventually degenerates until the committee is just happy to have a warm body filling every empty position. Often what members desire to do is not even a consideration, never mind finding out what their unique spiritual gifts might be. The idea of thirsting is ignored, which results in passionless and ineffective service. Yet another common, but equally fruitless way to get people to serve is the "Thank the Lord!" approach. When people do volunteer, they are handed minimal tools/materials to get the job done and are then sent on their way with a pat on the back and a great big thank you to the Lord. More often than not, they fail because no time or effort has been spent finding out what they desire to do, and then equipping them to do it. Tragically, when people fail for lack of training at something they are gifted for, they often give up on doing the very thing God has designed them for. When training is omitted, failure and discouragement are inevitable.

Yet a third mistake I see happening over and over again in ministry placement is called the "pass the buck" approach. When gifted people are burdened and then trained to serve, they deserve attention, support, input, and oversight from a leader in the church. So many times this just doesn't happen. People are placed in ministry and then forgotten. Leaders operate with an attitude of "It's their problem now" and absolve themselves of responsibility. Because there is no accountability—no one keeping track of the job—potential ineffectiveness isn't corrected and progressive error is not caught.

"This kind cannot come out by anything but prayer."

Mark 9:29

Moving from Equipped to Engaged | **DAY THREE**

Did You Know?

? **COMMON MISTAKES IN ENGAGEMENT**

- "Warm Body" approach: engages people where they may not be gifted or burdened, just to fill a slot
- "Thank the Lord" approach: engages people before they are ready because of the lack of workers
- "Pass the Buck" approach: engages people without continuing to give them oversight
- "Over the Shoulder" approach: engages people as assistants, but never lets go so they can have ownership and freedom.

This kind of engagement often results in painful and messy conflict down the road. Because the step of testing is omitted, problems are not corrected until they are large enough to catch everyone's attention. A biblical requirement of serving as a deacon is *"Let these also first be tested"* (1 Timothy 3:10). There is clearly mention of an official position of deacon in the New Testament, and this position is what Paul has in mind in this verse. The word *diakanos,* translated "deacon," literally means to serve. The principle of testing needs to be observed in all venues of service, not just for officers of a church. So what does this kind of testing look like?

📖 Read Luke 16:10.

What is the main point of this verse?

_____

_____

_____

_____

How does this relate to having a season of testing as someone moves toward engagement?

_____

_____

_____

_____

What is the benefit of finding faithfulness and unrighteousness when they are little?

_____

_____

_____

_____

_____

Doctrine

IMITATE CHRIST'S EXAMPLE

The Greek word for "imitators" in I Corinthians 11:1 is *mimetes,* from which we get our English word "mimic." While we are to follow the examples of godly leaders, we are only to imitate those things in their lives that line up with Christ. In Hebrews 13:7 we are told to imitate our leaders, but in 13:8 we are reminded, *"Jesus Christ is the same yesterday and today, yes and forever."* We are not to imitate everything about them, but only those things consistent with the unchanging example of Christ.

Luke 16:10 appears in the context of Jesus' parable of the unrighteous steward. This verse is about integrity and consistency. Our character will be revealed in small things as well as large. This idea shows us how important the principle of testing is, for if we do not test those who seek to serve, then we won't be there to see the small indiscretions and thus will be unaware of problems until the unrighteousness in small things leads to unrighteousness in large ones. The flip side of this is also true. Without testing, we miss the opportunity to observe small acts of faithfulness that make it easier to trust people with greater responsibility. Testing gives people the opportunity to prove themselves, whether for good or for bad, in less risky ways. But that is not the only benefit of testing.

📖 Look at the Scriptures on the next page and observe what they teach about spiritual growth and leadership development.

1 Corinthians 11:1

_____

_____

_____

_____

Hebrews 13:7

_____

_____

_____

_____

1 Thessalonians 1:5–7

_____

_____

_____

_____

In 1 Corinthians 11:1 the apostle Paul invites the Corinthian believers to *"Be imitators of me, just as I also am of Christ."* In other words, "follow me as I follow Him." Hebrews 13:7 adds further clarity to this concept, as we are told to consider the results of our leader's conduct before we *"imitate their faith."* This adds an important balance, for during this time of testing and development, we are learning from mentors, but we are not to imitate everything about them. Rather, we are only to imitate those things that are worthy. We see this idea played out to completion with the Thessalonian church. In 1 Thessalonians 1:5 we see Paul and company as examples (*"what kind of men we proved to be among you"*). In verse 6 we are told that the Thessalonians followed that example as *"imitators"* of their leaders to the point that in verse 7 we are told they themselves became *"an example to all the believers in Macedonia and Achaia."* Testing not only helps us to identify what people are, but also to develop their skills and character.

📖 Take a look at Galatians 2:1–10.

Why did Paul appear before those who were *"of high reputation"*?

_____

_____

_____

_____

How was this a period of testing in Paul's life?

_____

_____

_____

_____

What was the outcome of this meeting?

_____

_____

_____

_____

Galatians 2 recounts an important step in Paul's ministry. He appeared before the leaders of the mother church in Jerusalem to "double-check" his message—the gospel he was preaching—to make sure it was correct. What we see here is a clear picture of one operating under the authority of others, and even inviting their evaluation and feedback. This is what ought to happen in the step of testing. In this case, the leaders added nothing to Paul's message (verse 6), but the outcome was a clear affirmation of Paul and his ministry. Further, it lead to them giving Paul *"the right hand of fellowship"* in affirming his call to the Gentiles.

Testing is a necessary part of us identifying our course—the ministry the Lord has for us personally. What does testing accomplish? First of all, it helps leaders to weed out bad apples early. As we saw in Luke 16:10, *"He who is faithful in a very little thing is faithful also in much; and he who is unrighteous in a very little thing is unrighteous also in much."* If problems are recognized early on, they can be dealt with before much damage is done. Second, testing helps to correct mistakes and errors in the good apples before they create large messes and much discouragement. Leaders can help people be more effective and keep them from building bad habits. Third, testing makes it easier to spot emerging leaders and those with leadership potential as we see their faithfulness in little things. Fourth, testing helps us evaluate if a particular type of service is a good fit for a person or not. As we discussed in the previous lesson, one element of equipping is time, and the proven benefit that comes from time isn't just for the sake of seeing if someone is worthwhile or not. It also helps us prove what ministry one is best fitted for.

Testing allows for incremental service as gifts are developed and character proven. Testing also provides for further equipping as the servant learns how to implement skills through following the example of a leader. Further, testing provides needed evaluation and feedback, enabling those who lead to both affirm the servant as well as redirect him as needed.

Testing occurs naturally in apprenticeship relationships. We see this model of ministry development throughout Scripture. Jesus spent years developing the twelve before He deployed them. Often He would send them out for short-term assignments and then discuss what happened with them when they returned. Barnabas had this kind of relationship with the apostle Paul and with Mark who wrote the gospel that bears his name. Paul had such a relationship with Titus and Timothy and Silas. Even in the Old Testament we see men developed for service under the leadership of others. Joshua was an attendant to Moses for years before he was picked to replace him. If we are in leadership, we would be wise to provide such relationships to people before trusting them with a ministry of their own. If we are looking to find our personal ministry course, we need to seek out such leaders so we can be prepared for the work God has for us.

ENGAGEMENT LEADS TO ENTRUSTING

Finding our personal ministry course begins with thirsting. We must cultivate a desire to serve, and we must look for the desires for particular service that God places in our hearts. But desire is not the end of the journey. Rather, it is the beginning. To engage in effective service we must also be trained and equipped. In addition, we need to serve under the leadership of others in a season of testing. Then and only then are we ready for the step of entrusting—where God entrusts to us a successful ministry of our own. Sadly, many people never get that far in the process. Without proper training and guidance, they experience more failure than success and they give up. But there are success stories. In our own church, I see how significant it is when people make it through those steps and are engaged in effective service. They have joy and significance. They have fulfillment, and they make a difference in the lives of others. That ought to be what each of us aims for.

📖 Read Acts 18:24–28 and identify how many of the steps to engagement you can see demonstrated by Apollos.

Thirsting

_____

_____

_____

_____

Training

_____

_____

_____

_____

Testing

_____

_____

_____

_____

Trusting

_____

_____

_____

_____

STEPS TO FINDING YOUR COURSE

- Thirsting
- Training
- Testing
- Entrusting

All four steps of engagement are visible in the example of Apollos, though some are not stated as explicitly as others. We see thirsting in his passion for ministry (he is described as *"being fervent in spirit"* in verse 25, and he wanted to *"go across to Achaia"*—verse 27). Clearly he had desire. Second, we see training both in the fact that he had become *"mighty in the Scriptures"* (verse 24) and that he *"had been instructed in the way of the Lord"* (verse 25). We see testing evidenced in the instruction and correction he received from Priscilla and Aquilla (verse 26). And finally, we see entrusting in his being given encouragement from the brethren, as well as a letter of welcome (verse 27).

Apollos went on to serve effectively, verse 28 tells us. He *"powerfully refuted"* the arguments of the Jews against Jesus, and using their own Scriptures (the Old Testament), he proved Jesus to be the Messiah. We know from church history that Apollos went on to pastor both at Corinth and at Ephesus. Clearly he reached the stage of entrusting.

I don't mean to paint the picture as a precise step-by-step process, for there is some overlap between the stages. Sometimes it is through training or testing that thirsting is defined or refined. It is possible to be in training and testing at the same time instead of one preceding the other. In the same way, entrusting must not be painted as one step of finality. I may be trusted with several different ministries on the way to my ultimate destination in service. Such seems to be the case with Phillip, who was one of the seven pre-deacons of Acts 6, and who went on to become an effective evangelist.

📖 Look at Acts 11:24–26 and identify how Paul (Saul) was entrusted with a teaching ministry in Antioch.

_____

_____

_____

_____

When Barnabas was sent to Antioch to confirm if this work was of the Lord, he quickly saw the need for experienced laborers and went to find the apostle Paul. As a result of his sponsorship, Paul was entrusted with a teaching ministry there that had great impact. But for Paul to have that opportunity, someone with authority had to entrust him with the teaching responsibility. That same principle was in operation in Barnabas' life, for we see in Acts 11:22 that he had been *"sent"* to minister at Antioch by the leaders of the mother church in Jerusalem. Leadership plays a key role in this step.

📖 Identify from Acts 13:1–4 how Barnabas and Paul (Saul) were entrusted with their missionary ministry.

_____

_____

_____

_____

In Acts 13:1 we have a list of the leaders of the church at Antioch. As they were in a time of prayer, the Spirit directed them to *"'Set apart for Me Barnabas and Saul for the work to which I have called them.'"* It is important to notice that God did not reveal this call only to Barnabas and Saul. That all of the leaders were involved in affirming the call is evidenced by their laying hands on them and sending them out.

This passage shows a good portrait of the balance in the step of entrusting.

Did You Know?

BARNABAS AND PAUL

Generally, biblical lists move from most important to least. Most likely, the order of the list in Acts 13:1 indicates that Barnabas was the main leader of the church there and Saul (later named Paul) was a lesser of the associate pastors listed there, with the other leaders falling somewhere in between.

It is not man who sends or calls someone to serve. That is the work of God. But this work is confirmed when He reveals this call to those with leadership responsibility. The Holy Spirit calls, and leadership affirms. This distinction is more clearly seen in the Greek here than in English translations. In Acts 13:3, when we are told that the leaders at Antioch *"sent them away,"* the Greek word *apoluo* is used, which conveys the idea of loosing or releasing them to this ministry. In Acts 13:4, when we are told that they were *"sent out"* by the Holy Spirit, the Greek word *ekpempo* is used, which means "to send forth." The Holy Spirit did the calling and sending, and the leaders did the releasing and affirming. Both steps were necessary for the great missionary thrust of the book of Acts to become a reality.

Errors can be made in this step of entrusting. Leaders can err by trusting too soon those who are not yet proven or equipped. They can also err by being too slow to entrust or by never fully entrusting a ministry to someone. In many churches the ministry is limited because insecure and power-hungry leaders never let go of things and give freedom to called and qualified laymen. Without delegation, the ministry can never grow beyond what the pastor can personally manage. Laity as well can err with this principle of entrusting. If we do not wait for the affirmation of leadership, we can end up running ahead of God and missing His call. Or worse, we can run off on our own and rob ourselves of the resources, encouragement, and accountability of the church and its leaders. Everyone loses when this happens.

For Me to Follow God

How do we move from entry to equipped to engaged? Hopefully you appreciate the importance of each the four steps we have identified in the process of discovering the course the Lord has for us to follow. So why are those steps not always followed faithfully? There are many reasons. Leaders often don't follow the steps out of **impatience.** They see the steps as taking too much of the limited time they have. This makes sense in the short run, but it makes things harder in the long run, for if something isn't done right, it ends up having to be done over. Followers don't always follow the steps because of several reasons. One is **ignorance.** They haven't been educated to look at the proper steps, so with good but uninformed hearts, they omit important parts of the process. Another reason the steps aren't followed is **pride.** I have seen many people road-blocked in their attempts to have a ministry because their pride keeps them from seeing the need for training and accountability. Another reason the ladder that leads to engagement is not climbed is **unbelief.** You see, if we recognize entrusting as an integral component in the progression, we have to be willing to trust and to wait for God (and leadership) to open doors. We also have to be willing to trust God when those doors remain closed.

REASONS WHY WE DON'T RESPECT THE PROCESS OF ENAGEMENT

- Impatience
- Ignorance
- Pride
- Unbelief

Engagement is a work of God. He is the "placer." In fact, the Greek word for God ("*Theos*") literally means that. He is the One who gave us our gifts, He gives us our ministry, and He is the One who brings the results. Because of this, at every stage of the process we must keep our eyes on Him and be seeking His direction.

The first, and perhaps most important, application of this week's lesson is evaluation. We must begin by identifying where we are before we can know what we need to do next. Look at the list below, and fill in as many blanks as you can.

Thirsting

Do you have a desire to have a ministry?

_____

_____

If so, what type of ministry do you desire?

_____

_____

_____

If not, you need to recognize that it is God's will for you to have a ministry. What can you do to cultivate a desire?

_____

_____

_____

_____

Training

Training involves several steps. First (after salvation, of course) comes spiritual formation. This is training to walk with God. It involves things like learning how to pray, study the Bible, deal with sin, and other things involved in maintaining our fellowship with God. Next come the technical skills of our particular gifts and type of ministry. For example, if we feel called to teach, do we know how to prepare a lesson or guide a discussion? Third, we must gain experience in serving. Rate yourself in the different areas of training that are needed to minister effectively.

Spiritual Formation

Inadequate   1   2   3   4   5   Adequate

Technical Skills

Inadequate   1   2   3   4   5   Adequate

Ministry Experience

Inadequate   1   2   3   4   5   Adequate

What is your action plan to address the weak areas?

_____

_____

_____

_____

Training involves things like learning how to pray, study the Bible, deal with sin, and other things involved in maintaining our fellowship with God.

Testing

To whom are you accountable in your serving?

_____

_____

_____

Would you consider yourself "proven" to those in leadership at your church or ministry?

_____

_____

What steps can you take to gain affirmation of the leadership?

_____

_____

_____

_____

Who gives you feedback on the quality of your service?

_____

_____

_____

Entrusting

Entrusting is not synonymous with abandonment; it is instead an act of empowerment or transferring authority. The apostle Paul recognized a thirst to teach in Timothy. He personally trained him and tested him in a number of different ministry situations as they ministered together. Eventually Paul trusted Timothy with leadership over the church he had started in Ephesus. But that didn't mean Paul abandoned him. First and Second Timothy were written to continue advising Timothy and improve his effectiveness. You must understand that Paul wasn't there every day for Timothy to lean on. You may be at the point of entrusting, and if so, the questions below may help you make the most of your ministry. If you aren't there yet, just leave blank what doesn't apply.

What ministry or ministries do you feel you have been entrusted with by the Lord and leaders?

_____

_____

_____

_____

Are there any areas where you've stepped out without trust that need to be made right?

_____

_____

_____

> *Entrusting is not synonymous with abandonment; it is instead an act of empowerment or transferring authority.*

Are there any things you can do to gain trust and responsibility in your ministry area?

_____

_____

_____

_____

Accountability Commitment

Within the next month I will commit to taking the next step toward plugging into a place of service to the Lord. I recognize the body needs what I have to offer, and I need to offer my giftedness to the body as a faithful steward of what God has entrusted

Signed _____ Date _____

Close by writing a prayer expressing your heart to the Lord.

_____

_____

_____

_____

_____

_____

_____

_____

_____

_____

_____

_____

_____

_____

_____

_____

_____

_____

_____

The Secret Power of Serving

(1 CORINTHIANS 3)

Today we live in an electronic world, filled with ever-increasing technology. I wrote this Bible study on a notebook computer (that is literally as small as a notebook) with all the bells and whistles. It has far more power than computers that filled up an entire room in the 1960s and contains more information on its hard drive than all the shelves of books that surround me in my office. This computer I am using, as powerful as it is, will be a dinosaur in three years and probably extinct in six. But for the time being, it helps me accomplish a lot of work. I can write on it, search the internet with it, access a whole reference library off its hard drive, study Scripture passages in the original languages with the aid of software it runs, and even listen to music while I work. There is only one problem. With all the time, effort, manpower, and money that went into designing, manufacturing, shipping, distributing, and promoting this particular product, it is absolutely worthless unless it is connected to a source of energy. It can't do a thing unless I fully charge the lithium ion battery by plugging the cord into a wall socket. All that technology is of no benefit without power. Of course, any power tool doesn't accomplish the task it was designed for unless it is plugged in to its source of power.

In the same way, a Christian, even with all the right gifts and experience, even plugged into the right place of service, is not

"Apart from Me you can do nothing"

John 15:5

going to be effective at ministering and changing lives unless he is connected to and empowered by the Spirit of God. In John 7:38–39, Jesus told the people that if they believed in Him, *"From [their] innermost being shall flow rivers of living water."* The next verse clarifies what He said as a reference to the overflowing life of the Spirit. In Luke 24:49, Jesus told the disciples to tarry in Jerusalem until they were *"clothed with power from on high."* In Acts 1:8, just before Christ's ascension, He says, *"You shall receive power when the Holy Spirit has come upon you."* In all of these passages the message is clear: *"Apart from Me you can do nothing"* (John 15:5). For our service to have power, God must be working through us.

DAY ONE

THE PRINCIPLE OF POWER SERVING

My first foray into the arena of vocational ministry was in campus ministry. I had become a Christian in college through the ministry of Campus Crusade for Christ, and, a couple of years after graduation, I joined their staff with the University of Virginia as my first assignment. It was very different than the experience I had as a volunteer on my college campus. In fact, they don't call UVA a campus. It is formally referred to as "the Grounds." It is a prestigious and historic university founded by Thomas Jefferson and part of what is informally known as the "Ivy League of the South." I was expected to make contacts with interested freshmen, but there aren't any freshmen at this university. Students are identified simply as "first year," "second year," and so on. On my first trip to work, I parked my Toyota Tercel between a BMW and a Mercedes. As I got to know the students, I quickly learned that many of them had monthly allowances larger than my salary. One of the students I discipled had bought a house for his school years, while I could barely afford an apartment.

The affluence of many of the students was intimidating. What did they need from me? In addition to the challenges of working with kids who had everything, the University of Virginia was not very "ministry friendly." The administration was combative and did much to limit access to the students. We weren't allowed in the dorms without an invitation. Militant student groups like the Gay/Lesbian Alliance and Campus Atheists were constantly lobbying the student government in opposition to Christian organizations and causes. After one semester of trying to get some ministry going, I was seeing little progress and was ready to throw in the towel. One particular incident that fall remains vivid in my mind. I remember praying to the Lord and telling Him in great detail all of the reasons a Christian movement would never have any impact at that university. You see, I had been looking at the challenge in light of my meager personal resources, and I saw that they were lacking. It was a defining moment, for as I prayed, I sensed the Lord speaking to my heart: "Eddie, you can build the pile of reasons why it won't work as high as you want on one side of the scales, but I am on the other side." That one moment dramatically changed how I prayed for UVA. My attitude changed from doubt to belief, my supplication from complaining to asking. My most common prayer became, "Lord, never let me be satisfied with what I can do for You; let me see You do the things that only You can do." I stopped looking at my service as me working for God and began to recognize it as me walking with God and trusting Him as He works through me.

> "Lord, never let me be satisfied with what I can do for You; let me see You do the things that only You can do."

I was only at the University of Virginia for two years, but I got to see God do some incredible things. I shared the gospel widely as He opened doors. I saw future leaders trust Christ. I witnessed firsthand as the Lord changed lives and created in students a passion for the things of God. Our fledgling campus ministry more than doubled in size in those two years. We even started another campus ministry at nearby James Madison University that flourished and exposed the whole student population to the gospel in its first four years. Today, the young men I discipled there are scattered across the globe. Two went to Asia as missionaries and served in Taiwan and mainland China—one is still there. One serves with a mission group based in France that targets the Muslim world. One ministers in the research triangle of North Carolina with international students. One is the athletic director of a Christian college in the Midwest. Two are successful businessmen, making a difference for Christ in the corporate world. One is a pastor, and another works in Christian radio. But those are not things I did—God did them. There is all the difference in the world between us working for God and allowing God to work through us. Today we will begin looking at this issue of serving in God's power instead of our own.

📖 Read 1 Corinthians 3:10–15.

In this passage, Paul uses a building as an analogy for the Christian life.

What is the foundation of this building (verses 10–11)?

_____

_____

How, according to these verses, is this foundation laid? By whom is it laid?

_____

_____

_____

In verse 10, Paul uses the analogy of a building to explain the Christian life. Verse 11 tells us that the foundation of that building is Christ. There is no other place to start—there is no other way to begin. Christ is the foundation of our faith. Verse 10 tells us men lay this foundation; in this case Paul lays it. This is important, for God wills that His work be done through people. A building's foundation is "laid" only once, so this obviously is referring to salvation. The verse also tells us the means of this work. Paul says the foundation was laid *"according to the grace of God."* Grace, in this sense, is a synonym for God's power working through Him.

What does verse 12 teach us must be done with this foundation, and who must do it?

_____

_____

_____

The word *"builds"* in the Greek is in the present tense and active voice. The fact that it is in the present tense means that building on the foundation is a continuous, ongoing process. The active voice implies that the act of building is being performed by the subject, as opposed to someone doing it to him. Every believer has the responsibility of building a Christian life on the foun-

"Let each man be careful how he builds."

I Corinthians 3:10

dation of Christ in his heart. Salvation is to be more than mere fire insurance to protect us from hell, just as a building is to be more than a mere foundation.

📖 The list of building materials in verse 12 falls into two categories based upon the testing by fire of verse 13. Separate these materials into those two categories and write your observations about each.

_____

_____

_____

The building materials of verse 12 look pretty diverse until you put them in the context of verse 13. Then they fall quite neatly into two categories: one is valuable and the other, common. Gold, silver, and precious stones are obviously to be seen as one group, and wood, hay, and straw as another. When these two groups are tested by fire, one group can be destroyed by fire, while the other cannot.

📖 Verse 13 tells us a day is coming when the quality of our building will be tested. When will that test occur?

_____

_____

What is the tool used to test our works?

_____

All that Paul tells us here about when our work will be judged is that *"the day"* will reveal it. Notice that it does not say simply "a day," but *"the day."* Paul has a very specific day in mind. On this day to come, what is built on the foundation of Christ in our lives will be tested by fire.

In Paul's second letter to this Corinthian church, he wrote, *"For we must all appear before the judgment seat of Christ, that each one may be recompensed for his deeds in the body, according to what he has done, whether good or bad"* (2 Corinthians 5:10). Apparently that is the day he has in mind in the previous passage. This is not a judgment of the believer to determine his eternal destiny, for the apostle John wrote *"He who believes in Him is not judged; he who does not believe has been judged already, because he has not believed in the name of the only begotten Son of God"* (John 3:18). This judgment is not of the believer, but of his works, and only to determine reward.

What is the point of all of this? The main point is that not all service for the Lord is the same. Not all of our works make a lasting difference. This fact ought to catch our attention, for hopefully all of us want our works for the Lord here on earth to last.

The Secret Power of Serving   DAY TWO   # THE TESTING OF OUR WORKS

When I was a teen, one of the ways I earned some extra spending money was by helping to tear down houses and buildings. In the area where I grew up, there were plenty houses that needed to be razed because a hydroelectric dam was being built, and anything that the new manmade lake would cover had to be torn down. I got paid to help dismantle the condemned buildings, but I also learned there was extra money to be made on things we could salvage from the demolished buildings. We could pull out the electrical wires, and after burning the insulation off, we could sell the copper by the pound at the local scrap yard. They would also buy brass valves we reclaimed from the water pipes. The key to getting our money, though, was to remove all the steel and iron, because it wasn't nearly as valuable as the copper and brass. When we brought our scrap metal to the buyer, he would dump out our pieces of metal and then run a magnet over the batch to make sure the copper was solid and not just copper plated steel. He tested the quality of our metal before we were given our reward. The Bible teaches us that this is the same thing that Jesus will do with a believer's works. Knowing this ought to motivate us to be sure ours is the right kind of service.

📖 Look again at 1 Corinthians 3:10–15. There are two possible results of the test by fire as you can see from the categories we looked at yesterday. If our Christian lives are built from the first group of materials (gold, silver, and precious stones), when they are tested by fire, what will happen?

_____

_____

_____

_____

When gold, silver, and precious stones are put into the fire, they aren't destroyed. In fact, precious metals like gold and silver welcome fire. It removes impurities and makes them more valuable. A metal smith heats them until they melt into liquid, and then slag and impurities rise to the surface and can be skimmed off. He keeps working the metal, melting and skimming, until he can see his reflection. Then he knows the metal is pure.

📖 What will happen to the worker who has built with these first materials, according to verse 14?

_____

_____

_____

The worker who has built on the foundation of Christ with things that last receives a reward. The Bible speaks of our Christian reward in the form of crowns. It is significant that gold, silver, and precious stones are the materials crowns are made from.

📖 The second group of materials with which we can build our Christian life is wood, hay, and straw. The passage speaks of three results of testing this work.

1. What happens to this work when it is tested by fire?

_____

_____

Did You Know?

OUR REWARD

The Bible speaks of our reward as Christians in the form of crowns. The Bible identifies at least four different crowns for different acts of faithfulness:

1) the "crown of life" (James 1:12; Revelation 2:10)—for enduring trials;

2) The "imperishable" crown (1 Corinthians 9:25)—for running the race according to the rules

3) the "crown of righteousness" (2 Timothy 4:8)—for loving His appearing

4) the "crown of glory" (1 Peter 5:4)—for faithful church leaders.

Some argue for a fifth crown, the "crown of exultation" (1 Thessalonians 2:19)—for evangelism and discipleship, while others view this as being the same as the "crown of glory." The crowns will be used in heaven to worship Christ (Revelation 4:8–11).

2. What happens to the worker's reward, according to verse 15?

_____

_____

3. What about his salvation?

_____

_____

What are the three results from testing this work? **1)** When you put fire to wood, hay, and straw, it burns up, and nothing is left but ashes. Sadly, some people's Christian lives, though they may look busy and productive, are nothing more than big haystacks and are of no eternal consequence. **2)** We are told this person will *"suffer loss."* **3)** The one whose works are burned is still saved, but verse 15 adds, *"yet so as by fire."* Barrett says such a one is "as one who dashes through the flames safe, but with the smell of fire upon him." Ron Dunn calls it "saved, but singed." It is as if he gets as close to hell as one can without going there.

Today is the day of working, but tomorrow is the day of testing. Each of us will appear before the judgment seat of Christ so we can be rewarded for the deeds done in the body. Since we do not want to enter heaven empty handed, we must take care not only **that** we serve, but also **how** we serve. We want to build our reward with materials that will last.

The Secret Power of Serving

DAY THREE

DIFFERING WORKS WITH DIFFERENT RESULTS

Jesus, in the Sermon on the Mount, told a parable of construction. He said,

> _Therefore everyone who hears these words of Mine, and acts upon them, may be compared to a wise man, who built his house upon the rock. And the rain descended, and the floods came, and the winds blew, and burst against that house; and yet it did not fall, for it had been founded upon the rock. And everyone who hears these words of Mine, and does not act upon them, will be like a foolish man, who built his house upon the sand. And the rain descended, and the floods came, and the winds blew, and burst against that house; and it fell, and great was its fall. (Matthew 7:24–27)_

The principle here is the same as it is with Paul's analogy, though the application is decidedly different. Jesus' parable is about salvation; Paul's analogy is about reward. Jesus shows us there are two possible foundations for life—rock and sand—but only one of those foundations will last. Those who build their lives on any foundation other than Christ are not saved. Paul shows us that even if we choose the right foundation, we can still build the wrong way. The stakes are high. I don't want to build my Christian life with the wrong materials, but how can I know I'm building with the right ones? The answer is in the immediate context of the passage. There we see two categories of Christian experience that correspond to the two categories of building materials found in verses 10–15.

📖 Read 1 Corinthians 2:14—3:3 and record what you learn about *"spiritual men."*

_____

_____

_____

_____

Verse 1 of chapter 3 tells us Paul could not speak to the Corinthians as *"spiritual men."* At the end of chapter 2, Paul contrasts spiritual men with natural men, or unbelievers. In chapter 3, he contrasts them with *"men of flesh."* A spiritual man is a believer who is maturing in his walk and who is yielding to God in every area of life. In the Greek, the word for *"spiritual men"* literally means "spiritually with the assistance of the Spirit." It is the opposite of one who follows his fleshly nature. A spiritual man has discernment because he has the mind of Christ.

📖 The second type of believer Paul refers to is the man *"of flesh."* Verse 1 indicates that is what the Corinthians were. Look through the passage and write down what you glean about *"men of flesh."*

_____

_____

_____

_____

Are men of flesh believers? Paul says they are *"babes,"* but he also says they are *"in Christ."* A man of flesh would be a believer who has trusted Christ but is trying to live the Christian life in his own efforts. Verse 3 says they were *"walking like mere men"* (literally "according to man" instead of according to the Spirit). Such a one may still be trying to please God, but he is trying to do it through self-effort instead of by yielding to God. He may be working for God but not walking in His strength.

It is important to recognize that a believer can be in the flesh rather than walking in fellowship with God. It is also important to acknowledge that one who habitually lives a sinful life may not be a Christian at all. John tells us that no one who practices sin (as a lifestyle) is *"born of God"* (1 John 3:9). What Paul is addressing in 1 Corinthians 3 is the one who is a believer (*"in Christ"*) but is a babe, one who is not depending on the Spirit as he should.

Since there are two categories of Christian experience, it logically follows that there are also two categories of Christian service. The Spirit energizes the first type of service; this type is that which God does through us, that which is supernatural. When I'm yielded to God and have no conscious sin in my life that I haven't dealt with Him about, then He can work through me in supernatural ways. The second type of Christian service is based on **efforts** of the flesh. We try to serve and please God through self-effort. This kind of service is limited by man's abilities and is no different than what a non-Christian could do.

We must recognize that if there are two categories of Christian experience and of Christian service, then there will be two categories of results of Christian service. The first is **temporal** results. These are the works that have the appearance of spirituality but are of no eternal consequence because they are done by man's striving and self-effort. The second category of results is

Word Study
FLESH

There are two different but related Greek words translated "flesh" in the New Testament, *sarkinos* and *sarkikos*. Both come from the root word *sarx*, which conveys the idea of living flesh. The difference lies in the added endings. *Sarkinos* generally means flesh in the sense of "being made of matter," whereas *sarkikos* has more of an ethical meaning (propensities of the flesh unto sin). This is the word used in 1 Corinthians 3 in most manuscripts.

eternal results. These are the works wrought by God that will stand forever. If God does the work through us, then the results will always please God, even if they don't always please men.

📖 Look at Matthew 6:1–7, 16–18 and write down what you learn about the reward people get for service done with a wrong heart.

_____

_____

_____

In the Sermon on the Mount, Jesus addresses three different spiritual disciplines and shows how doing the right thing with a wrong heart does not produce eternal reward. Jesus addresses giving, prayer, and fasting. In each example, He confronts those who do such activities to be noticed by men and makes it clear that the only reward for service done in this manner is the applause of men. He contrasts this with these activities done with a right heart, and each time He makes the point that the Father who *"sees in secret"* will reward them.

God wants His children involved in good works. *"We are His workmanship, created in Christ Jesus for good works"* (Ephesians 2:10). But God cannot reward good works done from a fleshly heart and a desire to please men. The right thing done from a wrong heart isn't right at all, for God looks at the heart.

God cannot reward good works done from a fleshly heart.

The Secret Power of Serving

SERVING IN HIS POWER

I don't know about you, but I have sometimes wondered about Jesus' words in John 15:5, *"apart from Me you can do nothing."* There are two different ways Jesus could have said "nothing" in the Greek, and the one He chose means "not even one thing." I have seen a lot of people do a lot of things without Him, even religious things. But what I have not seen is people doing eternal things without Him. Using the analogy of John 15, the grape vine and its branches, what He seems to be saying is, "You might be able to make leaves, but you can't make grapes—not even one." Apart from the empowering work of God, we cannot produce fruit.

📖 There are two positive commands in the Bible regarding the Holy Spirit. The first is in Ephesians 5:18. Read it in its context and write your insights.

_____

_____

_____

In Ephesians 5:18, Paul commands us to be *"filled"* with the Spirit. The verb is a present imperative. The use of present tense indicates that we are not just to be filled for a moment, but as a way of life. The imperative mood of this verb means it is a command, not a suggestion. To be filled with the Spirit isn't like filling an empty glass with water. We got all of the Spirit we are going to get when we became Christians. The issue isn't getting more of the Spirit, but the Spirit getting more of us. To be filled with the Spirit is to have no area of life closed off from Him. Instead of filling an empty glass with water, it is more like dropping an Alka-Seltzer into the water. It is pervaded from the inside out. The first step to being filled with the Spirit is to **confess** the sin of directing your own life and **repent**. The Greek word for "confess" means to "agree" with God. He calls something sin; we agree with Him. If we truly agree with Him about our sin, there will always be repentance. If we are unwilling to repent, we don't really agree that we are wrong. Being filled with the Spirit doesn't mean we will never fail, but that we will never fail to deal with it when we do.

The second step to being filled with the Spirit is to **surrender** control of your life and ministry to Christ. In order for our service to have power, it must be yielded to God, and we must trust Him to empower it. If we've been running our own lives and ministries, there will be no power and lives won't be changed. Surrender doesn't mean asking God to bless our ideas; it means laying down our ideas and seeking God's will. There is no surrender without seeking the will of God, and there is no discerning the will of God without surrender. The two go hand in hand.

📖 Look at Galatians 5:16.

What does it say we are to do in relation to the Spirit?

_____

_____

What are the results of this?

_____

_____

_____

_____

Here Paul says we are to *"walk by the Spirit."* He tells us if we do, we will not fulfill the desires of the flesh. In this same chapter, Paul speaks of the *"fruit of the Spirit"*—nine character qualities that obviously cannot be produced in our own strength or else we wouldn't need Christ.

Walking by the Spirit, or allowing His control in our lives, first means moment-by-moment dependence and trust (faith). A real danger to true power serving can be our training and experience. Having them is great but if we're not careful, the more of them we have the more our trust is in them instead of God. Sometimes it's harder to trust God in our strengths than our weaknesses.

Secondly, walking by the Spirit means keeping short accounts with God about your sin. Walking by the Spirit doesn't mean we stop sinning altogether. That won't happen until heaven. What it means is that when we do sin, we deal with it right away. We don't let sin stay in our hearts for any length of time. Sin short-circuits God's power in our lives, and if we don't deal with it, there will be no power in our service. Psalm 139:23–24 is a good model of how to keep short accounts with God: *"Search me, O God, and know my heart; try me and know my anxious thoughts; and see if there be any hurtful way in me, and lead me in the everlasting way."* That should be a regular prayer in our lives, inviting God to show any sin to be dealt with.

"*And do not be drunk with wine, in which is dissipation; but be filled with the Spirit,*"

Ephesians 5:18

We have seen the proper way of relating to the Spirit. There are also some sins to avoid in order to stay yielded to God. The first is in Acts 7:51. Read the verse in its context, identify the wrong posture toward the Holy Spirit found there, and write what you think brings it about.

_____

_____

_____

_____

_____

_____

One who resists the Spirit is one who, because of spiritual blindness, works against God, not for Him. Resisting the Spirit is a lack of surrender to Christ's Lordship and leading because of rebellion or ignorance (not seeing what God is doing). Blindness to the work of God occurs when we allow unconfessed sin to remain in our hearts.

The second sin is found in Ephesians 4:30. Read the verse in its context and write your observations.

_____

_____

_____

_____

One who *"grieves"* the Spirit (causes sorrow to the indwelling Spirit of God) is one who chooses to do something he knows is not God's will. The Holy Spirit is grieved when we commit an act of sin that we know violates what God has said not to do.

Look at 1 Thessalonians 5:19 for the third sin and write what you learn.

_____

_____

_____

_____

The word *"quench"* means "to put out a fire." The Spirit is often symbolized with fire, and we cool His fire in our life and ministry when we refuse to step out in faith and trust Him in what He has called us to do. We must guard against these three sins—resisting, grieving, and quenching the Holy Spirit—if we are to serve God with power as He desires.

Doctrine

A RIGHT RELATION TO THE SPIRIT

DO

■ be filled with the Spirit

■ walk by the Spirit

DON'T:

■ resist the Spirit

■ grieve the Spirit

■ quench the Spirit

The Secret Power of Serving

DAY FIVE

FOR ME TO FOLLOW GOD

The Spirit of God takes up residence in our lives at the moment we become Christians. In 1 Corinthians 6:19, Paul tells us that our bodies are *"temple[s] of the Holy Spirit."* Worship is honoring the Lord with our choices and submitting to His Spirit living in us. Our worship and our service are affected negatively when we resist the Spirit, grieve the Spirit, or quench the Spirit. The secret to power serving is to keep the Lord in control of our lives and on the throne of our hearts. In a word, the key to power serving is surrender. It is saying to the Lord, "I can't, but You can." I can teach, but I can't change lives. I can give, but I can't empower that giving or give to the right place in the right way without God and His leading. I can show mercy, but I can't do it with balance without the Spirit's leadership. The power of every gift is not in the gift itself, but in the giver. Apart from Him we can do nothing of value or consequence.

 Are there any areas in your walk and ministry where God has let you see that your dependence and trust isn't focused on Him but on your own strengths?

_____

_____

_____

_____

Nothing is more frustrating than long-term service in an area where you are not gifted. Ephesians 4:7 tells us that *"to each of us grace was given according to the measure of Christ's gift."* He guarantees us the grace needed to fulfill our gift and/or calling. If we aren't consistently experiencing the grace, we may not have the gift or calling. On the other hand, sometimes even if we are serving in the right place, we are frustrated because we are trying to do the work in our own efforts instead of allowing Christ to do it through us. It is essential that any service we offer be done not in fleshly, human effort, but by the energizing power of the indwelling Spirit. Consider the following questions as you evaluate your present or past service.

1. Do I understand the SPIRIT-FILLED LIFE adequately enough to be able to discern between self-effort and Christ working through me?

_____

_____

_____

Do I sense that I'm trying too hard in my service, or do I sense God's power channeled through me to fulfill the tasks of my ministry?

_____

_____

_____

_____

Is there any evidence of the supernatural (motivation, energy, results, etc.) in what I do?

_____

_____

_____

_____

> The power of every gift is not in the gift itself, but in the giver. Apart from Him we can do nothing of value or consequence.

2. Does my present service flow out of how God has GIFTED me?

Am I gifted in ways suited to the tasks of my ministry?

_____

_____

_____

Does my service reflect good stewardship of my gifts?

_____

_____

_____

_____

3. Is there a sense of PERSONAL BURDEN for my area of service?

Do I sense that what I am doing really needs to be done?

_____

_____

_____

_____

Is there a deep concern over the area of my service?

_____

_____

_____

_____

In Their Shoes
PAUL'S LIFE

The life of the apostle Paul gives us a good picture both of serving in the flesh and serving in the Spirit. His life and ministry before he met Christ on the Damascus road portrayed religious zeal. He was outstanding among the Pharisees and was the prime mover in the persecution aimed at ridding Israel of the sect of Christianity. He was working hard for God, but was actually working against Him. After he met Christ, his ambition switched from trying to have a righteousness based on his own keeping of the law, to a pursuit of a righteousness based on faith (Philippians 3:9)—trusting God instead of himself.

4. Is there a clear sense that God has CALLED me to this ministry?

Was the opportunity and leading for this service initiated by God, or manipulated by me?

_____

_____

_____

Do I feel that God really wants me to do what I am doing?

_____

_____

_____

_____

5. Do I have a growing DESIRE to serve the Lord in this way?

Do I enjoy my present venue of service?

_____

_____

_____

Does my service provide a sense of fulfillment and satisfaction?

_____

_____

_____

6. Is there evidence of FRUITFULNESS in my service?

Do I see fruit in others as a result of my service?

_____

_____

_____

Do those to whom I minister affirm my contribution?

_____

_____

_____

Are you effectively serving in the proper place? Determining this is more than merely judging how you feel at any particular moment. It takes evaluating the long-term pattern. How you answered the questions above may show you a change is needed in where you serve, or they may show you a change is needed in how you serve. If you feel you need help serving in the right way, seek the guidance of the Spirit. If you sense a need for change, seek counsel and direction from ministry leaders for a place of service more in line with how God has gifted and burdened you.

Close out this week's lesson by putting what God has shown you into a written prayer.

_____

_____

_____

_____

_____

_____

_____

_____

"For we are the true circumcision, who worship in the Spirit of God and glory in Christ Jesus and put no confidence in the flesh."

Philippians 3:3

Barriers to Serving

Why don't all Christians have a ministry? The Bible clearly states that we should. God has given each of us a spiritual gift. He wants us to employ that gift in serving one another. So why are some believers content to be spectators, while others find themselves overworked, over-stressed, and underappreciated? Is it simply an issue of sin? In the average church, less than ten percent of the congregation fills all the volunteer roles of service. In some churches, that number is as low as five percent. Does that mean everyone else is disobedient to God? This is one question we must consider. We would have to assume that some do not serve out of sinful, selfish reasons. But that alone does not explain the disparity between gifted people and engaged servants. Some of the blame must lie elsewhere.

For some, serving the Lord is inhibited not by sin, but by imma-turity. They simply haven't matured to the point of being ready to have a ministry—they are still in the state of being ministered to. While some stay in spiritual infancy too long, it isn't wrong for someone to focus on personal growth before moving into ministry. Others do not serve because they do not yet know the Lord. Unbelievers should not be serving, for they will do so for the wrong reasons—working for a relationship with God instead of from it. For these reasons alone, the church will never

Why don't all Christians have a ministry? The Bible clearly states that we should.

have one hundred percent of the congregation engaged in serving. But there are other reasons people don't serve, and many of those reasons are inexcusable. Many times, the church itself is to blame for the inactivity of its members.

Many years ago, before becoming chaplain of the U.S. Senate, Richard Halverson was pastor of the First Presbyterian Church in Hollywood, California. One day a leading layman who had recently been elected president of the local school board approached him. This layman related to the pastor that because of his added responsibilities, he would need to drop some of his church commitments. At first, Pastor Halverson was upset at the thought of losing so active a worker in the church. Here are some of his reflections:

> As I pondered the loss of this fine young man . . . I asked . . . 'How many do we need to really do the work of the organization of this church?' . . . Many of the men and women in the church had several jobs. . . . They were very busy with the ecclesiastical establishment. But suppose that each could hold only one job. How many would it take to do the work of that large congregation? At the time, the membership was about seven thousand. To my amazement, I found that it would require only 365 to do the work that was required to maintain the program of the First Presbyterian Church of Hollywood. . . . This meant that most of the members of the church could never have a job in the institution. It followed . . . that if the work of the church is what is done for the institution, very few, relatively speaking, will ever have an opportunity to do the work of the church. (Richard C. Halverson, *How I Changed My Thinking About the Church,* Grand Rapids: Zondervan Publishing House, 1972, pp.73–74)

In this major church, it only took about 5 percent of the membership to fill all the roles of serving in the church—and the pastor was having a hard time finding that five percent!

The church needs workers. Larry Richard and his colleagues asked five thousand pastorswhat the greatest needs are for strengthening the church. On a scale of one to five, from a twenty-five item list, nearly one hundred percent gave a first or second priority to "getting my lay people involved as ministering men and women" (as quoted in *Unleashing the Church,* Frank R. Tillapaugh, Regal Books, 1982, p. 20). Yet the Church must accept some of the blame for its inability to motivate people to serve. One of the reasons people don't serve is that the Church has not created enough opportunities for them to serve. Perhaps the Church has wrongly defined true ministry as only that which happens inside the walls. Another reason is that the Church has not adequately equipped people to serve, creating a profound negative affect in the following ways:

Under-equipped people do not have the confidence to serve
Under-equipped laborers often fail when they do serve.

Furthermore, when under-equipped Christians continually lose confidence after each failure, they sometimes give up on serving all together, concluding that they just don't have what it takes.

The problem of people failing in service is not caused by one single culprit; therefore, there is no single solution. In this lesson, we will look at some of the barriers we face when engaging in ministry and what to do to remove them. We also will consider some of the mistakes we make that hinder our service.

THE NEED FOR ENDURANCE

What gets in the way of people serving? One problem I have observed is "the logjam effect." I am reminded of a recent hunting trip where I made my way to a favorite spot, only to discover that this prime location was now completely under water. What used to be a nice, dry spot near a creek was now a waist-deep pond. Beavers had moved into the area and dammed the creek. My friend who owns the land had to take immediate action, for much of this land is used to raise pine trees to sell as pulpwood. Unless the water was drained, the trees would die. It took some labor on his part to burst open the beaver dam and let the water drain. In many ways, logjams hinder the Church. For whatever reason, we have an army of laborers held back from serving, and it is going to take some effort to break through the logjams that are keeping people from doing what God created them to do. The need of the hour is not finding someone to blame, but finding solutions. Problem solving requires understanding the many different hindrances to ministry.

📖 Read Hebrews 12:1–2

What is the main call for us in these verses?

_____

_____

_____

What barriers must be overcome to do what we are called to do?

_____

_____

_____

Word Study
THE RACE

In Hebrews 12:1 of the original Greek, the word translated "race" is a definite article. Thus this verse speaks of "a particular or specific race." God has mapped out a race for each of us to run as believers.

The opening verses of Hebrews 12 call us to run *"the race"* that is set before us. It portrays the Christian life as a marathon. Yet to succeed in this assignment, we must lay aside *"every encumbrance"*—in other words, everything that slows us down as we run. We must also lay aside sins that entangle us, tripping us up as we run. Third, we must run our race *"with endurance"*—we must not grow weary and drop out. Finally, we must fix our eyes on Jesus, who both originates and completes our faith.

Think about the message of these verses as it relates to why people don't serve. Some aren't ministering because they are encumbered, slowed down by things in their lives. Others don't serve because of entanglements of sin. Still others, though they are serving, are ineffective because they are misguided and not properly focused. And some have lost their endurance and dropped out of service entirely. Whatever the reason, many people are missing out on the satisfaction and significance of serving in the way God created them. *"We are His workmanship, created in Christ Jesus for good works that we should walk in them"* (Ephesians 2:10). We will never find satisfaction apart from being who God made us to be and doing what He made us to do.

The Field of Fatigue
Hebrews 12:1 tells us we are to *"run with endurance"* our personal race. One of the barriers to serving is what I call "the field of fatigue." *Webster's*

Dictionary defines fatigue as "exhausting effort or activity." There is nothing wrong whatsoever in growing weary **in** the work, but something is definitely wrong if we grow weary **of** it. As we saw in the previous lesson, we are called to serve in His strength, not our own.

📖 Look at Acts 1:8. What does Jesus say will be the result of being controlled and directed by the Holy Spirit?

_____

_____

_____

Jesus instructs, *". . . you shall receive power when the Holy Spirit has come upon you."* The world is not impressed with what we do for God in our own strength. All religions involve working for God. What separates Christianity from other religions is that it involves God working through us.

📖 What does 1 Peter 4:11 say about how we are to serve?

_____

_____

_____

Peter tells us that whoever serves is to do so *"by the strength which God supplies."* If we serve in our own strength, we will inevitably grow weary of the work. One of the reasons I call this "the field of fatigue" is that I picture a long flat area where I can see how far I have to go—how much more there is to do—and I want to give up. As a teenager in East Tennessee, one of the jobs I did to earn money was to help farmers put up their hay. It was exhausting, sweaty, backbreaking work, and sometimes, in the middle of the field, it looked like we would never finish the task. Serving in the Church in our own strength will only motivate us to give up. If we do give up, the memory of our collapse will be a barrier to ever serving again, even though the problem may not have been the place of service but the fatigue of serving in our own energy.

Fatigue is a problem for the individual, but church leaders can add to the problem. Our leaders must teach people how to serve in God's strength and not their own. They must also recognize that part of engaging people in ministry is promoting a vision. The "thrill" of working in the nursery or the parking lot is not enough motivation for most of us to see its value. We need leaders to build bridges between the trivial things we place value upon and the treasured things we don't properly appreciate. A gentleman saw two bricklayers at work and went up to the first one and asked, "What are you doing?" The man unenthusiastically responded, "I'm laying bricks." The gentleman asked the same question of the second man and got a totally different answer. "I'm building a cathedral for people to worship God!" the second laborer passionately replied. The men were performing exactly the same task, but the difference was one of vision. The second man was able to see what his contribution meant to the whole. One bricklayer had temporal vision, while the other bricklayer had relational vision. One man's vision terminated at the end of the task. The other man's vision enabled him to relate his task to the greater goal.

Most of us don't get excited about correcting our vision. It is the job of leadership to help us think relationally—to relate our tasks to the overall objec-

Our leaders must teach people how to serve in God's strength and not their own.

tive. Nursery work may sound unattractive if we think only of crying babies and messy diapers. But the task is totally transformed when you can grasp a vision of a young mother worshiping God without the distraction of a crying and fidgety baby that would only have hindered her worship and the worship of those around her. Parking cars may not in itself seem very significant or eternally valuable, but when one can see the grand picture of helping visitors connect to a place where they can hear the Word of God and grow spiritually, suddenly the task seems more honorable. When we look at the grand scheme of God's work, we are able to associate temporal activities with eternal values.

One of the things that gets in the way of engaging is when leaders try to recruit people to a task with terminal thinking: "We need someone to work in the nursery today—there are thirty screaming babies over there and only one worker!" It would take a pretty strong dose of mercy for someone to get past that visionless presentation of a chance to minister. Probably the only ones who would respond would be those who already had vision for the value of the task. This kind of engaging is what I would call "mercy engaging"—only God's mercy makes it work at all!

Leadership must see need differently. Often engaging is hindered because the only needs leadership sees are the immediate vacancies to be filled. The biblical reality is that every member of Christ's body needs a ministry. We need to give out of service, whether or not there is a need in the nursery. Engaging looks not just at the ministry need, but the minister's need. Leaders can unintentionally become a barrier to people serving if they aren't careful. Since leaders are usually the ones who open doors for people to serve, they can create barriers with an inflexible structure or by offering only limited opportunities. They can also build barriers if they allow the congregation to remain ignorant of opportunities for service.

THE BARRIER OF ENCUMBRANCES

Barriers to Serving **DAY TWO**

When I attended East Tennessee State University back in the 1970s, the school boasted a nationally ranked track and cross country team. The program was consistently competitive and boasted such greats as Neil Cusack, a Boston marathon winner, and Ray Flynn, one of the fastest milers in the world. Can you imagine Neil trying to run a marathon in a business suit wearing wingtips and carrying a brief case? As great a runner as Neil was, it is doubtful he would finish a race in such attire, and it is certain he wouldn't win. What if Ray Flynn tried running the mile in a wetsuit and flippers? These athletes could not hope to succeed with such encumbrances.

In Hebrews 12:1, we are instructed to *"lay aside every encumbrance."* The Greek word for encumbrance (*ogkos*) refers to "a weight," "a burden," or "an impediment"—in other words, something that slows us down. It isn't speaking of something sinful as much as something that hinders us and keeps us from being effective. One of the reasons some people don't involve themselves in ministry is because other situations encumber them. It could be the myriad of details that complicate and clutter their lives. These burdens could be the very things that distract their attention from God, from important priorities, from their course or race. Or they could be the events that fill their time and keep them from being able to do God's will.

The Ditch of Indecision

As I have observed people over the years, I have seen that many are kept from having a ministry because they never cross "the ditch of indecision." It isn't that they actively decide not to serve the Lord. It is just that they never decide at all. To fail to decide is, by default, a negative decision. Sometimes we are so busy (too busy) with things that aren't all that important that we are unable to say "yes" to things we should be doing. We never commit to serve.

📖 Carefully read 2 Timothy 2:4 and write down what you learn about encumbrances.

_____

_____

_____

_____

_____

The apostle Paul exhorts Timothy, *"No soldier in active service entangles himself in the affairs of everyday life, so that he may please the one who enlisted him as a soldier."* A soldier has to deal with everyday life the same as anyone else. He must eat. He has to brush his teeth and floss. He has to do laundry and polish his shoes. But a soldier doesn't allow himself to become entangled in things that keep him from doing his job. His motivation is to please the one who enlisted him as a soldier. If our motive is to please the Lord, then we cannot let encumbrances keep us from serving.

Just as a ditch must be crossed to get to the other side. if you and I are ever to engage in ministry, then it will mean deciding to say "yes" to an opportunity to serve. Maybe we don't need to sign up for the rest of our lives, but everyone must start serving somewhere. What I see is that for most people, their service is general in the beginning. The longer they serve, however, the more specific their ministering becomes and the more it fits them personally—their gifts, passions, and personality. But they will never progress if they never decide how they are gifted.

The River of Fear

Another encumbrance that keeps people from serving is "the river of fear." They are hindered by personal insecurities and inadequacies. President Teddy Roosevelt once said, "You'll never lead a cavalry charge if you think you look funny sitting on a horse." All of us have insecurities and feelings of inadequacy, but if we wait to serve until we are perfect, we never will. What fears keep us from serving? Fear of failure, fear of looking foolish, fear of getting in over our heads, fear of what people think of us—these are just some of the phobias that hinder us. Perhaps our fears aren't unfounded and are showing us a need for more training. Maybe our fears are rooted in a lack of experience. If so, it is okay to start slow and small. Maybe we lack confidence because we know what we are supposed to do but we haven't had the chance to observe someone else do it. We need a model. Whatever the reason for our fears, we cannot allow them to keep us from serving. We need to remove the source of those fears where we can, and it may be that the source is simply a lack of faith.

"No soldier in active service entangles himself in the affairs of everyday life, so that he may please the one who enlisted him as a soldier."

2 Timothy 2:4

📖 Take a look at Paul's advice to his disciple, Timothy, in 2 Timothy 1:7 and make note of how it relates to our serving.

_____

_____

_____

_____

Paul wrote this particular letter to Timothy from prison near the end of his life. His passion in writing this letter was to aid Timothy, his disciple, who was now serving as the main leader of the church at Ephesus. He counsels Timothy, *"God has not given us a spirit of timidity."* Fear is an emotion, and as such is a free agent. It can say whatever it wants. We can't keep the emotions from showing up, but we can choose to surrender those feelings to the Lord. If we are timid in our serving, it isn't from Him. What is from Him—and what we can have if we ask for it—is *"power and love and discipline."*

📖 Make note of how Proverbs 29:25 relates to our serving.

_____

_____

_____

_____

"The fear of man brings a snare." If we are too worried about what people think to be concerned with pleasing the Lord, we have already become ensnared. What is the solution to fear? Is it to avoid the thing we fear? No. The solution to fear is to trust the Lord. Andrew Jackson once defined courage in this way: "Courage is not the absence of fear, but the willingness to do the thing you fear."

A river can be a fearful thing. Whitewater rapids aren't easy to cross. But if we will trust the Lord, He will become a bridge to get us to the other side. The river of fear is another obstacle that must be crossed, because fear is an encumbrance that can slow us down. It isn't a sin to be afraid, but it can become sin if our fears keep us from trusting the Lord and obeying His instruction. We must lay aside every encumbrance if we are to run the race He has for us.

> *"For God has not given us a spirit of timidity, but of power and love and discipline."*
> 2 Timothy 1:7

THE BARRIER OF ENTANGLEMENTS

Barriers to Serving DAY THREE

We have asserted in this lesson that one reason people do not serve is fatigue. They grow weary when they serve in their own strength, and this short-circuits future serving. We also learned that another barrier that keeps God's people from engaging in ministry is encumbrances—the weight of indecision or the burden of fear. Attitudes of fear and fatigue are not sinful when dealt with appropriately. Yet such attitudes can keep us from obeying the Lord's instruction to employ our gifts in serving one another, and disobedience is clearly sin. We will now look at a third barrier to serving. Some are not serving the Lord because of sin in their lives. They have become entangled—tripped up in their race by the chains of sin. As a result, they are not running their race. In the 1984 Summer Olympic Games in Los Angeles, the American Mary Decker was considered a sure bet for the gold medal in her distance event, the 3000 meters. Yet halfway through the race, her feet became entangled with those of South African Zola Budd, and she tripped. Not only was she denied the gold medal, but she didn't even finish the race. Sadly, a great many believers are not finishing the race because they are tripped up by sin.

The Desert of Compromise

Webster's Dictionary defines compromise as "a concession to something that is harmful or depreciative." It is hard to serve God when you are entangled in sin. Ask believers who have spent any time in this predicament, and they will tell you that compromise with sin and worldly pursuits is indeed a road that leads to desolation. "The desert of compromise" is a dry and forsaken place where one can easily get lost.

The Lord appointed Samson to be a judge. He was meant to be a deliverer of his people. But Samson had a problem. He had a wandering eye when it came to women. He married a pagan Philistine because *"she looked good to Samson"* (Judges 14:7). That marriage was a disaster, and almost cost him his life, but he did not learn his lesson. The next compromise was a relationship with a harlot from Gaza, and again, he barely escaped with his life when the Gazites heard he was there (Judges 16:1–3). Still, his weakness remained unchecked. Next, we find him in the arms of Delilah. Even when he realized she was trying to trap him, he continued the relationship. But before he recognized it, he was entangled in the cords of sin, and his compromise became costly indeed. It cost him his vision, his ministry, his freedom, and in the end, his own life. Sin will take you further than you thought you would stray, keep you longer than you thought you would stay, and cost you more than you thought you would pay. Just look at Samson's example. He tasted firsthand the desert of compromise.

📖 Consider Paul's words in 2 Timothy 4:10 and write down what you learn about Demas.

_____

_____

_____

_____

In some of the last written words of the great apostle, we have recorded the failings of his ministry companion, Demas. In Philemon 1:24, Demas is referred to as a *"fellow worker"* of Paul's, along with Mark, Aristarchus, and Luke. He is mentioned as well in Colossians 4:14 as sending his greetings to that church along with Paul and Luke. But in 2 Timothy 4:10, we read, *"for Demas, having loved this present world, has deserted me and gone to Thessalonica."* He abandoned Paul in his hour of need because he became entangled in the sin of worldliness. In our lives as well, sin and worldly pursuits can become an entanglement that must be laid aside.

The Swamp of Lethargy

Not long ago, I visited the great Everglades of southern Florida. I traveled with others deep into the swamp at dusk by airboat. It was quite an adventure for me, but even more of an adventure for those who chose not to stay in the

At a casual glance, it appears that Samson escaped from Gaza with no consequences for his sin. That is probably how he interpreted it. But looking more closely, we see that this stepping across the line of immorality (sleeping with a harlot) kindled his lusts and took him further than he intended to stray.

Did You Know?

CAST YOUR CARES UPON GOD

Paul's mention of Demas *"having loved this present world"* in 2 Timothy 4:10 is probably an intentional contrast with 2 Timothy 4:8. There, Paul speaks of the reward of the *"crown of righteousness"* that is given to *"all who have loved His appearing."* We either love this world or the world to come.

boat. When some of my crew ventured into the water, they quickly became mired in deep, oozing mud. I learned from their mistake, so I didn't have to repeat it. Unfortunately, many believers are kept from making a difference in ministry because they have stepped out of the boat of God's will and have become trapped in the mud of spiritual laziness and selfishness. Some do not serve because they love money, pleasure, and self more than they love God. They are too wrapped up in their selfish pursuits to realize they are trapped by them. *Webster's Dictionary* defines laziness as "resisting exertion, work or other activity." My paraphrase is "doing what you want to do (sometimes nothing) instead of what you ought to be doing." Spiritual laziness is really an oxymoron, for to be lazy is contrary to being spiritual and is associated with being selfish. I discovered that the Everglades is one large, stinky swamp where people can get stuck in the mud. Being stuck in a state of selfishness is a similar predicament. Because the appetite of flesh is never satisfied when we live selfishly, neither can we be satisfied. We rob ourselves of contentment and significance, and we rob others of the blessing God wants us to be in their lives. One of the manifestations of selfishness is pride. Often it keeps us from serving because we think something unworthy of us or too insignificant. What we fail to realize is that Jesus led by being a servant. Without the attitude of servanthood, we will never be great in the kingdom. If our pride keeps us from serving where the Lord gives us opportunity, then while seeking to be what we consider significant, we make ourselves eternally insignificant.

📖 2 Timothy 3:1–5 mentions four different "lovers." Look at the text and identify each of these and how they stand in contrast to each other.

_____

_____

_____

_____

_____

_____

Paul warns us that in the last days there will be four different kinds of "lovers": lovers of self, lovers of money, lovers of pleasure, and lovers of God. The first three stand in stark contrast to the fourth. They exist in the company of those who are *"boastful, arrogant, revilers, disobedient to parents, ungrateful, unholy, unloving, irreconcilable, malicious gossips, without self-control, brutal, haters of good, treacherous, reckless, conceited."* We were made to be lovers, and we will be. Either we will love God, or we will love something else. One of the things that keeps people from serving is that they love self, money, and pleasure instead of loving God and their neighbor.

Ask Jonah about the entanglement of selfishness. God called him to take the message of repentance and forgiveness to the pagan Ninevites. But instead, he ran the opposite direction. From Jonah's example, we learn that you can run from God, but you can't escape Him. When you run from Him, you run back into Him. Jonah fled on a ship, so God chased him with a storm. But still Jonah was selfish. He chose suicide over obedience. He was cast into the sea, having gone down every step of his journey. He went *down to Joppa* (Jonah 1:3), and then when the storm came he went down into the hold of the ship (Jonah 1:5). When he went overboard, he went down into the belly of a great fish (Jonah 1:17) who took him down into the depths of the sea (Jonah 2:2). He lost his joy, his testimony, his compassion for others (i.e., the lives of the sailors he had put in jeopardy), and he almost lost his life. But if

Did You Know?

❓ **JONAH**

Jonah was a prophet to the Northern Kingdom of Israel from 793 B.C. to 753 B.C., during the reign of Jeroboam II. Little is known of him except the events recorded in the book of Jonah..

there is one thing we learn from the example of Jonah, it is that God is committed to our having a ministry. He is going to do whatever it takes to pry us loose from the swamp of lethargy. Like Jonah, some of us are weathering storms in our lives right now because we are running from God. Jonah's example tells us to repent and obey.

Fortunately, the story of Jonah doesn't end with the fish. When he cried to the Lord from the belly of the whale, God answered him and delivered him. He obeyed and went to Nineveh and saw the greatest revival recorded in Scripture. An entire city, estimated to be inhabited by more than a million people, turned to the Lord. It is never too late to repent of our selfishness and obey the Lord's call to serve.

Hebrews 12 instructs us to lay aside *"the sin which so easily entangles us."* The sins of worldly pursuits and selfishness are entanglements which must be laid aside. When we do so, the Lord will accomplish great things through us that will benefit many others. We dare not rob the Church of what God wants to do through us.

Barriers to Serving

DAY FOUR

Fixing Our Eyes on Jesus

Doctrine

RUNNING THE RACE

How do we run the race of the Christian life? Hebrews 12 gives us four keys that all begin with the letter "E":

■ Encumbrances laid aside

■ Entanglements laid aside

■ Endurance as we run

■ Eyes fixed on Jesus

One of the observations my wife makes about my driving is that it is dangerous for me to look at anything beside the road, for as soon as I do, the car starts drifting from my lane of traffic. I'm not exactly sure why it happens, but I have to agree that it does. I'm not convinced, though, that it only happens to men, as my wife suggests. My theory is that it happens to husbands more because they can't get their wives to drive on trips. It isn't a good excuse, but it is the best I have been able to come up with so far. One of the factors that inhibit effective serving is taking our eyes off of Jesus. As soon as we do, we stray from the course He has for us, and we end up doing things other than what He has called us to. Jesus says in Luke 9:62: *"No one, after putting his hand to the plow and looking back, is fit for the kingdom of God."* His point was taken from a commonly observed principle in agriculture: the only way to plow a straight line is to keep your eyes fixed on something on the horizon. If you look back, you can no longer plow straight. Hebrews 12 tells us that the only way to run our race effectively is to fix our eyes on Jesus.

The Forest of Frustration

A forest is a dark place where you can get sidetracked. Have you ever been lost in a deep forest? It is surprisingly easy. I remember one particular time I was out hunting wild game. I had hiked into the woods along a high voltage power line where the ground was cleared and the walking was easy. When I reached the area where I wanted to hunt, I hiked straight into the forest. After ten minutes of walking in what I thought was a straight line, I found myself back at the power line. I was amazed, and somewhat frustrated, though at least I wasn't lost anymore. But in the woods, with uneven ground and longer vision blocked by the trees, it is easy to become disoriented. This is why many hikers and wilderness explorers depend on compasses and the latest global positioning satellite (GPS) equipment to keep them in the right direction. Without equipment of this type or any orienteering skills, those entering the deep woods may be headed for a heap of frustration. Speaking of frustration, *Webster's Dictionary* defines it this way: "to prevent from obtaining a goal or fulfilling a desire." Sometimes on the way to finding our course in life, we get sidetracked by opportunities to serve that do not fit us and our gifts. I call this barrier "the forest of frustration." Serving outside our giftedness is neither satisfying to us, nor is it usually effective. Part of knowing who you are and where you fit is knowing who you are **not** and where you **don't fit.**

📖 Look at Matthew 11:28–30 and identify how what Jesus said relates to our serving.

_____

_____

_____

_____

_____

Jesus says in Matthew 11:30, *"My yoke is easy and My burden is light."* But if we are carrying the wrong burden, it won't be easy. We don't normally think of these verses in the context of serving, but the principle certainly applies. We can find ourselves weary and heavy laden when we are carrying a burden that is not God's plan for us. The solution is to come to Jesus and find rest.

The Mountains of Work

When Lewis and Clark set out on their expedition to explore the Louisiana Purchase, their goal was to find a route through the Rocky Mountains to the ocean. They presumed that if they climbed to the top of the mountains, they could find streams on the other side that could be navigated all the way to the sea. But when they reached what they thought was the crest of the Continental Divide, they discovered not a steady downhill trek to the sea, but peak after peak of more mountains, and they knew immediately that their task was going to be much more daunting than they first thought. These mountains that mystified Lewis and Clark are a picture of the mountain-size barriers that can obscure our view of the course. One such barrier that keeps some believers from serving today is the overwhelming nature of the task at hand. When we see the mountains of work ahead of us, we can become so discouraged and intimidated by all there is to do that we do absolutely nothing.

📖 Read Matthew 9:37–38 and write your thoughts on how this relates to the "mountains of work."

_____

_____

_____

_____

MATTHEW 9:37–38

Jesus instructed us to *"Beseech the Lord of the harvest to send out workers into His harvest."* As we beseech God, we will be sensitive to His sending us to our place in the harvest fields. We must keep our eyes fixed on Jesus, not upon tasks.

Jesus said in Matthew 9:37, *"The harvest is plentiful, but the workers are few."* There will always be more work than we can accomplish. That is why it is essential that we run only the course that God sets before us and not try to run everybody else's course. We must run our course wisely. It is interesting to note Jesus' solution to this problem of the harvest being too great for the workers; He instructs the disciples to pray about it. *"Beseech the Lord of the harvest to send out workers into His harvest."* Why did He not say, "Hey, you guys, get to work!"? Because we must be sent. As we beseech God, we will be led to our place in the harvest fields. We must keep our eyes fixed on Jesus, not on the tasks.

📖 Take a look at Matthew 14:22–33.

What was Peter able to do with his eyes fixed on Jesus (verses 28–29)?

_____

_____

_____

What happened to Peter when he took his eyes off Jesus (verse 30)?

_____

_____

_____

What application does this hold for us in light of what we have been considering?

_____

_____

_____

_____

When Jesus came to the disciples walking on the water in Matthew 14, Peter said, *"command me to come to you on the water,"* and He did. You must not miss that point. Peter was not able to walk on water until Jesus called him. Once he was called, as long as his eyes were focused on Jesus, Peter was able to walk on the water like Jesus. But when he took his eyes off of Jesus and focused on the wind and waves, he began to sink. We cannot let the overwhelming nature of our work obscure our view of Jesus, or we will be overcome.

Hebrews 12 makes it clear that the way to run our race is by fixing our eyes on Jesus. He is the author (originator) and finisher (completer) of our faith. This phrase, *"fixing our eyes,"* literally means, "look away to." It means to look away from one thing and to concentrate on another. If we wander into the forest of frustration, we must fix our eyes on Jesus to find our way back to our course. If the mountains of work overwhelm us, we must not focus on the work, but on Jesus. Then and only then will we see the work in its proper perspective.

Barriers to Serving　　**DAY FIVE**　　# FOR ME TO FOLLOW GOD

Every believer is supposed to have a ministry, but not all do. For years, church leaders have told people they should serve, but often haven't told them why, shown them how, or given any practical solutions to the barriers that are preventing them from serving. The first step toward solving this dilemma is identifying the specific problem. Today we will focus our application on helping you to do that and suggesting what to do next.

We identified seven barriers to effective engagement in ministry. What presents a problem for one may not be an issue at all for another. Take a look at each of these and evaluate which are relevant to you. Place a checkmark in your book beside ones you know fit you, and then concentrate your efforts there.

SEVEN BARRIERS

Seven barriers to effective engagement in ministry:

■ Fatigue

■ Indecision

■ Fear

■ Compromise

■ Lethargy

■ Frustration

■ Burnout

The Field of Fatigue

Because a field is long and flat, you are able to see how far you have to go. Fatigue may motivate you to give up. The key is to replenish your strength by drawing on His strength. Isaiah 40:31 reminds us, *"Yet those who wait for the LORD will gain new strength; they will mount up with wings like eagles, they will run and not get tired, they will walk and not become weary."*

 Do you sense you are not serving in an area because you were burnt out in the past?

_____

_____

_____

What would you say caused your burnout ? (Check one.)

___ serving in the wrong place

___ serving in the right place, but in your own strength

If you checked the first one, commit to research places of service that fit your giftedness, and share that commitment with your pastor or church leader. If you checked the second one, you may need to review last week's lesson on "The Secret of Power Serving." Remember, Hebrews 12:1 says we must run our race with endurance. Hebrews 12:3 shows us how to run with endurance: *"Consider Him who has endured such hostility by sinners against Himself, so that you may not grow weary and lose heart."* "Consider Him" is an aorist imperative verb in the Greek. This means each and every time we are weary and tempted to lose heart, we are commanded to think of Him.

The Ditch of Indecision

Most believers have never made a conscious choice not to serve. It is simply that they have never decided at all. As you look at your own situations, check the items that are relevant.

___ I have decided that I am going to serve somewhere. (If you can't place a check for this statement, explain why in the space below.)

_____

_____

_____

___ I have not actively investigated the opportunities to serve that fit me.

___ I have opportunities to serve that interest me, but haven't made a decision.

How do we come to a place of decision about opportunities to serve? First we must decide once and for all, "I will serve somewhere." If we have done that, we can trust the Lord will guide us to the right place. The next step is to investigate. Make an appointment to discuss the matter with your spiritual leader. If you have multiple opportunities but can't decide, seek a trial period in each. Walk in the light that you have, and the process of walking will give you more light.

"For consider Him who has endured such hostility by sinners against Himself, so that you will not grow weary and lose heart."

Hebrews 12:3

The River of Fear

Fear is a natural human emotion. It makes us take serious things seriously. But it can also cause us to make lame excuses for not serving. We must face our fears and deal with them one by one. The only thing the Bible ever tells us to fear is God. We don't have to be afraid of what He will do, but we should fear disobeying Him and displeasing Him. Check the fears listed below that are holding you back.

❏ I fear failing

❏ I fear looking foolish

❏ I fear getting in over my head

❏ I fear what people will think

❏ I feel unworthy

Other_____

Now, go back through the ones you checked and place a number beside it from the solutions below that you think fit your situation.

❏ I need further training

❏ I need to see the right way to serve modeled

❏ I need to gain some experience with feedback

❏ I need to trust the Lord with this fear

The Desert of Compromise

A desert is a dry and barren place. Compromise with sin can make our spiritual lives a desert. First John 2:16 puts all sin into three categories: *"the lust of the flesh"* (sensualism, love of pleasure), *"the lust of the eyes"* (materialism, love of money and things), and *"the boastful pride of life"* (love of self, ego). Check which of these compromises is hindering effective service in your life?

____ lust of the flesh
____ lust of the eyes
____ boastful pride of life

The solution to compromise is two-fold. First you must confess and repent. Agree with what God says about that sin. Call it wrong, call it off, and call it forgiven. Second, yield that area to the Lord. You cannot conquer sin. If you could, you wouldn't need a Savior. The solution to sin is not us conquering it, but Him conquering us.

The Swamp of Lethargy

Many a believer is bogged down in the swamp of lethargy. Selfishness and worldly pursuits are keeping them from serving as they should. This is similar to the desert of compromise, but with this danger it is necessary to look not just to actions that are sinful, but attitudes that are wrong and must change.

 What are some selfish things that you are putting ahead of serving the Lord?

_____

_____

_____

_____

_____

Are you selfish with your time?

_____

One of the solutions to spiritual laziness is truth—studying the Word of God to change our beliefs. Acquiring truth will lead to changes in our behavior. Another practical solution is to look at our time like we do our money. Do you give a tithe of your money to the Lord? Do you tithe your time as well?

 Look practically at what it would mean to give the Lord ten percent of your time for worship and service.

What would it mean to give the Lord ten percent of your time for worship and service?

The Forest of Frustration
Have you lost your way in the harvest fields of ministry? Is the yoke you carry heavy or light? Do you think you are carrying the right yoke?

_____

_____

_____

_____

Remember, the solution is to fix your eyes on Jesus. You may need to spend some time seeking Him for direction. If so, involve others in that process. Seek counsel and prayer support.

The Mountains of Work
Are your eyes on the task instead of the Lord? If you have been focusing on how much work there is to do, you are probably overwhelmed. The problem could be one of the following situations. Check the statements that apply.

___ I don't have a clear sense of calling for what I am doing

___ I am in the right place, but need others to labor with me

___ I am seeing too much of the need and not enough of the Savior

Whichever of these statements best describe you, the solution is the same. Earnestly ask the Lord of the harvest to send forth laborers into His harvest. If you don't have a clear sense of calling, pray for Him to "send" you. If you need the help of other laborers, pray for Him to raise that help up. If you are overwhelmed by how much there is to do, pray, and remember it is HIS harvest. Let Him carry the weight of responsibility.

 As we close this week, review the barriers that relate to you and the applications you sense the Lord initiating, and express these to Him in a written prayer.

_____

_____

_____

_____

_____

_____

Spiritual Gift Wrapping

(1 CORINTHIANS 13)

Gift giving is a big part of our culture. We give gifts at Christmas, for birthdays, for Valentine's Day, anniversaries, Mother's Day, Father's Day, and just about every other day that is special. One thing gifts often have in common is that they are wrapped to look attractive and to be presentable. We have been studying the subject of gifts—spiritual ones—and did you know they are supposed to be wrapped as well? Every single passage that addresses spiritual gifts mentions love either immediately before or after (or both). The lengthiest treatment of spiritual gifts is found in 1 Corinthians 12. At the end of that chapter Paul concludes, *"And I show you a still more excellent way"* (12:31). He then moves into the "Love Chapter" (1 Corinthians 13). The Romans 12 list of gifts (12:3–8) is followed immediately by these charges: *"Let love be without hypocrisy"* (12:9) and *"Be devoted to one another in brotherly love"* (12:10). The 1 Peter 4 list (4:10–11) is preceded by the exhortation, *"Above all, keep fervent in your love for one another, because love covers a multitude of sins. . . . Be hospitable to one another without complaint"* (4:8–9). In the context of Paul's gift list in Ephesians 4:7–16, we find these challenges: *"showing forbearance to one another in love"* (verse 2), *"speaking the truth in love"* (verse 15) and *"...for the building up of itself in love"* (verse 16). What is the appropriate wrapping for spiritual gifts? Of course, the answer is love.

"But now abide faith, hope, love, these three; but the greatest of these is love."

1 Corinthians 13:13

When the apostle Paul made his short list of the things that would last (1 Corinthians 13:13), he identified only three things: faith, hope, and love. Even within those, he identified that love was the greatest of the three. In that same passage Paul identified several things that would not last. *"Gifts of prophecy,"* Paul informed us, *"will be done away." "If there are tongues, they will cease; if there is knowledge, it will be done away."* Often in our spiritual lives we major on those things that are temporary instead of those that are permanent. We think maturity is reflected in the supernatural or in the super-spiritual. We think if we knew more than anyone else, or could speak the mind of God, or could speak with other languages, we would really be something. Paul makes it clear that there are more important things than those that are temporal. They may not be flashy, but the things that will last are really those things that are most important.

Over the course of these last few lessons, we have looked at faith as a practical measure of our maturity. How willing are we to trust God—to take Him at His word? We looked at hope as another measure of spiritual maturity. Do we keep in focus the future promises of God for us and do we allow that focus to affect how we live today? The final member of this triad is love, and Paul calls it the most important of the three—"the greatest." God has called us to a life of love. He has called us to be like Him. Listen to the words of the apostle John: *"Beloved, let us love one another, for love is from God; and every one who loves is born of God and knows God. The one who does not love does not know God, for God is love"* (1 John 4:7–8). God <u>IS</u> love. Love isn't merely something God does; it is part of who He is. We are never more like God than when we truly love.

Word Study

LOVE

The Greek language had four different words for love . . .

Eros: Erotic or sensual love

Philia: Friend love or friendship

Storgē: Parental love

Agapē: Unconditional love, love of God

THE PRIORITY OF LOVE

There is a tendency in spiritual circles to think that others (and therefore, God) should be impressed by how much we know. Information equals godliness and spiritual value. We might not say it in those terms, but this terse message is preached loudly by how we live. Another tendency is to think that others (and therefore, God) should be impressed by how gifted and talented we are. The fact that giftedness equals importance is the unspoken message here. But neither of these messages in itself is affirmed by the Bible. In fact, it is quite the opposite. James tells us that we should prove ourselves doers of the Word and not merely hearers *"who delude themselves"* (1:22). In layman's terms, knowledge alone deludes us or deceives us into thinking we are spiritual because of how much we know instead of how we live. In 1 Corinthians 8:1, Paul wrote, *"Knowledge makes arrogant, but love edifies."* The apostle Paul spoke extensively of spiritual giftedness in 1 Corinthians 12, but he closed out the chapter by saying, *"And I show you a still more excellent way"* (verse 31), and spent the whole next chapter talking about love. Do you get the point? Love is what really matters in the Christian life.

When something is emphasized over and over as being of great importance, it is essential that we identify what it is and what it isn't. The English term "love" has been so cheapened by overuse that by it we can mean anything or nothing at all. We "love" God, but we also "love" potato chips. Yet the language of the Bible was not so careless with the term. In fact, there are four different Greek words for love. The one we speak of when we speak of God's love is the word *agape*. It describes God's unconditional commitment to us—which seeks to benefit us by doing what we need. It is selfless love, and stands in stark contrast to everything else we call love.

When Paul wrote to the Corinthian church, he wrote to a group of Christians that was out of balance. Their church services were pure chaos with everyone trying to put in their two-cents worth. They lacked neither knowledge (1:5), nor spiritual gifts (1:7), yet they were far from godly. Paul was trying to re-educate them about the proper place and function of spiritual gifts, yet in the midst of this discussion, he spent an entire chapter talking about love, or as he called it, the *"more excellent way."* Let's look at what he says.

Read 1 Corinthians 13:1.

What special gifts does Paul speak of here?

_____

_____

What is their impact without love?

_____

_____

Word Study

SENSELESS NOISE

First Corinthians 13:1 says, *"If I speak with the tongues of men and of angels, but do not have love, I have become a noisy gong or a clanging cymbal."* In the culture of Corinth, a noisy gong was usually associated with the "Copper Bowl of Dodona" at the oracle of Dodona. It was said to sound all day long and therefore was used to describe a person who talked incessantly. This cultural insight suggests that eloquence without love is not only empty noise but also annoying.

The Corinthian church members prided themselves in their ability to speak in unknown tongues. A unique supernatural manifestation of God's power first occurred on the day of Pentecost, when travelers from other nations miraculously heard the gospel message in their native languages. Although such phenomena are mentioned several times in the book of Acts, speaking in tongues was never the main emphasis of the early church. Yet it apparently had become the main emphasis in Corinth. Paul makes it clear that speaking in the tongues of other men or even in the heavenly tongue of angels is nothing more than senseless noise if it is not accompanied by love.

Take a look at 1 Corinthians 13:2.

What gifts are mentioned here?

_____

_____

_____

_____

What is their result without love?

_____

_____

_____

_____

In verse 1, Paul spoke of one of the "sign" gifts—a supernatural gift that points us to God. Here in verse 2, Paul mentions several of what are known as the "foundation" gifts. These are the gifts upon which the early church was founded. The gifts of prophecy, knowledge, and faith are essential for a church to be birthed; however, a foundation built with these three gifts is structurally flawed without love. Gifts without love accomplish nothing, and Paul goes one step further to say that without love *"I am nothing."*

📖 Take a moment to consider what Paul says in 1 Corinthians 13:3.

What gifts and service are mentioned here?

_____

_____

_____

What is their result without love?

_____

_____

_____

_____

Think of what Paul says here. If I give away everything I own, but my motive is anything other than love, there is no profit in it. I will not be rewarded spiritually for such actions. Even if I am a martyr, but my offering of myself is without love, my sacrifice makes no real difference.

Love is superior to the supernatural; it is superior to the spiritual; and it is superior to the sacrificial. Paul is not putting down gifts here, but elevating love. He is not saying knowledge is bad. We need knowledge, but not knowledge by itself. Love without knowledge is deficient, but knowledge without love is dangerous. They must both be exercised. If we call the divine abilities to serve one another "spiritual gifts," then perhaps love should be called "spiritual gift wrapping." All that we do must be wrapped in love or our service will not make a difference.

Spiritual Gift Wrapping

DAY TWO

THE PRACTICE OF LOVE

We often tend to think of love as an emotion. We think of the great passion with which Romeo loves Juliet. While love produces very strong emotions, it is far more than just emotion—it is action. The apostle John was at first known as one of the "sons of thunder" (Mark 3:17), yet Jesus made such a difference in his life that he came to be known as the apostle of love. He referred to himself as the disciple whom Jesus loved. John was so gripped by the love of God for him that he couldn't help expressing that love toward others. He wrote, *"We love, because He first loved us"* (1 John 4:19). But again, this love that John describes is not just emotion, but also a course of action. He also wrote, *"Little children, let us not love with word or with tongue, but in deed and truth"* (1 John 3:18). In other words, "Don't just say it, show it." John could say this because his life backed it up. As we continue looking at 1 Corinthians 13, we want to consider not just the priority of love, but the practice as well.

📖 Read through 1 Corinthians 13:4–7 slowly and reflectively. Now as you go back through it, look at the two things from verse 4 that love "is." What do you think these words mean?

Love is patient

_____

_____

_____

Love is kind

_____

_____

_____

While much practical application can be gained by thinking on the meanings of these words in English, even more can be learned from the meaning of the original Greek words. The Greek word for "patient" is *makrothumeō*, from *makro* (long) and *thumos* (wrath or anger). It means to be long or slow to get angry. It is used to communicate the idea of being patient with people, rather than with circumstances and situations. We are loving someone when we are patient with them and slow to get angry. The word "kind" is from the root word *chrestos*, which means useful or beneficial. We are loving someone when we seek to benefit them and to be useful to them.

📖 Look at 1 Corinthians 13:4–7 and identify all the things it teaches us that love **is not** or **does not do.**

_____

_____

_____

_____

_____

_____

_____

Sometimes it is most helpful to define what a thing is by defining what it is not. Here Paul spends considerable time doing just that. He tells us first of all that love *"is not jealous."* Jealousy or envy has the idea of comparing our lot to what someone else has. We are marked by self-centeredness if we cannot rejoice with what someone else has without wanting it for ourselves. Another thing that love is not is boastful or bragging—thinking too highly of oneself. Pride is at odds with real love, leading directly to the next negative verb Paul mentions: love is not arrogant. The Greek word for arrogant (*phusioō*) literally means "to inflate or puff up" and is used to describe a braggart or "windbag." The word figuratively portrays the idea of one who is always trying to make himself or herself out to be more than he or she is. This is a mark of one who loves self, not of one who loves others.

Love *"does not act unbecomingly."* The Greek word for "act unbecomingly" (*aschēmoneō*) literally means to behave in an ugly, indecent, unseemly or unbecoming manner. Love does not intentionally cause disgrace to another, nor does it *"seek its own"*—in other words, it does not put self first. Love *"is not provoked"*—it is not easily aroused to anger. As we can quickly see, the kind of love God calls us to have for each other is very different from the kind of sappy, valentine-like emotions that we hear of in love songs and love stories. True love, we are told here, *"does not take into account a wrong suffered."* The Greek word for "account" (*logizomai*) was used of financial reckonings. In other words, love isn't always keeping score and recording debits and credits to bring up in the future. Finally, love does not rejoice in unrighteousness. At first glance, this **"does not"** of love may seem a little out of place, until you think about it. Essentially, the point Paul makes is that love is so committed to a person's best, that it is unable—even if one cares deeply for the other—to find any joy in another's wrongdoing. To truly love someone means we are willing to point out wrongs to that person, not ignore that person or join in wrongdoing.

When you understand all that love is not, you begin to see how beautiful this kind of love really is. Each of us longs in the deepest recesses of our being to be loved like this. Paul says that we ought to start by showing such a love to others. How do we do that? By dealing with the "don'ts" as they show up in our lives, turning away from them toward what love calls us to do.

📖 Read through 1 Corinthians 13:6b–7 and identify the positive commands of these verses.

_____

_____

_____

"Love does not rejoice in unrighteousness, but rejoices in the truth." We are not loving someone when we cheer them for doing wrong. We love them when we speak truth, even if it is the truth of rebuke. Proverbs 27:5–6 tells us, *"Better is open rebuke than love that is concealed. Faithful are the wounds of a friend, but deceitful are the kisses of an enemy."* We are being loving when we speak truth for someone's good, even if it will wound him or her. As believers we can rejoice only in truth. Paul goes on in verse 7 to tell us that love *"bears all things"* (love is supportive), *"believes all things"* (love trusts that the motives of action are pure—it thinks the best of others), *"hopes all things"* (where error is seen, love hopes for change), and *"endures all things"* (bears up patiently). Love has this indefatigable capacity to endure in spite of the ingratitude, bad conduct, and problems that eventually show up in any relationship that continues long enough. Love is action—love is something we do, not just something we feel.

Spiritual Gift Wrapping

The Permanence of Love

"**T**ill death do us part"—I've heard these words more times than I can count. You probably have too. Every wedding is marked by vows of permanent love. Yet sadly, not every marriage is permanent. Why is that? I would suggest that many marriages today are built on the shaky foundation of emotions instead of the bedrock of commitment. Now, I am no marriage expert, but I do see a lot of marriages come and go. I am a pastor, and I do my share of pre-marital counseling, wedding ceremonies, and marriage counseling. What I try to point out from the very beginning is that it is commitment that produces abiding emotions, not the other way around. Emotions are like "free agents" in the world of professional sports; in other words, they can change teams at a moment's notice. But a decision to commit can keep those emotions coming back to a place of abiding. That principle is true for marriage, and it is also true for all our relationships in the body of Christ. But most of all, it is true of God's love for us. Because we have been adopted into His family, God has made a permanent commitment to us. He will love us no matter what we do. Because God is eternal, and God is love, God's love is eternal. Gifts will end. Love will not. Therefore, our acting in love toward others should have no end either. In a world of broken promises and broken hearts, God wants His people to be marked by the permanent love that He is.

📖 Read through 1 Corinthians 13:8.

What do you think it means that love "never fails"?

_____

_____

_____

Why do you think Paul mentions the things that he says will not last?

_____

_____

_____

_____

_____

_____

Love never fails. Is that really true? It is if you understand "agape" love. What Paul is saying here is not that human love will never let us down, but that when we love with God's love, that love will always accomplish the purpose God intends. In other words, God's love always works—even when nothing else does. It is interesting that Paul mentions in this verse three things that won't last, and each of them—prophecy, tongues, and knowledge—was apparently something the Corinthians thought a lot about and tried to emphasize in their church. To paraphrase, Paul says, "You are focusing on something that is temporal when you ought to be focusing on something permanent: Love."

📖 What do you think verses 9–10 mean in contrast to love?

_____

_____

_____

_____

_____

We saw that the gifts are passing. Here Paul shows us that they are also partial. They aren't complete. They aren't enough by themselves. The whole purpose of spiritual gifts is to enable us to love here and now. The gifts are a means to an end, not the end itself. But a day is coming when such tools will no longer be needed. In the presence of Christ, love will still matter but gifts won't.

📖 Why do you think Paul talks about growing up in this context (1 Corinthians 13:10–11)?

_____

_____

_____

_____

Paul seems to be saying, "We will outgrow the gifts, but not love." The gifts serve a purpose in the present, but not in heaven. The gifts that so enamored the Corinthian church were the sign gifts—those gifts that point us to Christ. In heaven, we will be in His perfect presence, and there will be no need to point to Him. Yet for eternity, love will still be relevant. Love knows none of the limitations mentioned of the gifts in these verses. The virtues listed in verses 4–7 outlast any gift and are to be cultivated earnestly.

Spiritual Gift Wrapping

DAY FOUR

THE PRODUCT OF LOVE

When we face death, the sobering knowledge that our time on earth is fleeting tends to reduce the concerns of life to matters of most importance. Trivial matters are quickly discarded. When Jesus faced His own death, His conversations with the disciples were anything but trivial. The gospel of John devotes five chapters to all that Jesus said and did the night before His arrest and crucifixion. Over the course of that evening, three times Jesus repeated a specific command. The context of the command alone speaks of its significance. In John 13:34, Jesus said, *"A new commandment I give to you, that you love one another, even as I have loved you, that you also love one another."* In John 15:12, He repeated, *"This is My commandment, that you love one another, just as I have loved you."* And again, in John 15:17 He told them, *"This I command you, that you love one another."* By now, you should be getting the idea that love for others is something Jesus feels strongly about. Why is Jesus so concerned that we love one another? Well, for one thing, He wants us to be like God, and God is love (see 1 John 4:8, 16). Another reason is that we all need to be loved and we need not be focused only on ourselves. Christ has liberated us from being slaves of self. Ironically, God has designed life in such a way that when we focus on self, we become isolated, but when we forget self, the deepest needs of our hearts end up getting met. God wants us to be agents of love. If we are, such displays of love will have a positive impact upon the lives of others and we will be blessed well for being obedient to God's greatest commandment.

📖 Look at John 13:34–35.

What does Jesus command us to do (verse 34)?

_____

_____

_____

_____

_____

"Love never fails."

1 Corinthians 13:8

What does He say will result if we do (verse 35)?

_____

_____

_____

_____

Jesus didn't suggest that we love one another; He commanded it. In fact, He called it a *"new commandment."* The Jews were very familiar with the idea of commandments, and they were very proud of the Ten Commandments God had given to Moses on Mount Sinai. But in their zeal to obey the letter of the law, they had neglected the most important commandments: to love the Lord and to love others (Matthew 22:37–39). Jesus tells us in verse 35 that it is by our love for one another that others will see the reality of God in us. The great Christian apologist, Francis Schaeffer, called love "the final apologetic"—the final proof of Christianity. It is not our morality that convinces the unbelieving world that God is real. It is our ability to love.

📖 Read 1 Corinthians 8:1.

What is the result of knowledge?

_____

_____

_____

What is the result of love?

_____

_____

_____

Often we think, *If I knew everything, I would really be somebody.* But it is clear from this verse that knowledge alone doesn't make someone better or useful. When Paul says that knowledge *"makes arrogant"* the Greek term literally means, "knowledge puffs up." It inflates our view of ourselves like a balloon, which looks big because it is full of air but has no real substance. Love, on the other hand, instead of making us arrogant, makes us useful. Love "edifies." The word means to build others up. Love always benefits others.

📖 Take a look at 1 Peter 4:8.

What are we instructed to do?

_____

_____

What will result when we do this?

_____

_____

_____

_____

Did You Know?

(?) **THE GREATEST COMMANDMENT**

God gave Israel ten commandments written on tablets of stone and delivered to Moses. By the time of Christ, Jewish rabbis had expanded those ten commands into 642 laws the people were expected to keep. Yet Jesus said that the whole law is fulfilled in two commandments: love God with all your heart, soul, mind and strength, and love your neighbor as yourself (Matthew 22:37–40). He reduced the 642 laws of men to one word: love.

Love is not the only thing Peter instructs believers here to do, but it is the most important. *"Above all"* he instructs, we are to keep fervent in our love for each other. One of the results of a life of loving is that love will make up for many offenses. Each of us makes mistakes. We are all flawed and prone to failure. Some of those mistakes will hurt others. But if our lives are characterized by *agape* love, then it will be easy for others to overlook our mistakes. Love covers a multitude of sins.

Think about what we have learned today. Love makes a difference. It makes an impact wherever it is shown. It proves to the unbeliever the reality of Christ. It builds up other believers with whom we interact, and it makes up for our own failings. No wonder the Bible makes such a big deal about love.

DAY FIVE

FOR ME TO FOLLOW GOD

One of the measures of our spiritual progress is how we do at caring. God has called us to love, and what He calls us to do, He has enabled us to do. He gives us the ability to love. The apostle John wrote, *"We love, because He first loved us"* (1 John 4:19). It is our own experience of God's love that enables to be an agent of that love to others. God's love is not like human love. He loves us not because of who and what we are, but in spite of who we are. In turn, He enables us to love, not just the lovely, but the unlovely as well. The apostle Peter wrote, *"Let all be harmonious, sympathetic, brotherly, kindhearted, and humble in spirit; not returning evil for evil, or insult for insult, but giving a blessing instead"* (1 Peter 3:8–9). How well we do at loving our neighbor says much about how far we have come in our spiritual life.

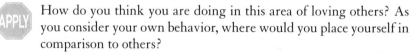 How do you think you are doing in this area of loving others? As you consider your own behavior, where would you place yourself in comparison to others?

☐ Less loving than others
☐ About the same
☐ More loving than others

Having asked you that question, I must quickly confess that it was a trick question. In fact, I think that very question is part of our problem. You see, the measure is not how I compare to those around me. My calling is not simply to be as good or better than those around me. It is to be like Christ. The right question is not "Do I love like others?" but "Do I love like Christ would?" How would you rate yourself in that?

_____

_____

_____

Christ fulfilled 1 Corinthians 13 to the letter. If God is love, then God in the flesh would be the model of love. If we want to be like Him, then this chapter ought to show us where we are weak. Look through the fifteen verbs below that describe love and identify the two or three you feel are most evident in your life and the two or three you feel are most lacking as well.

> "Let all be harmonious, sympathetic, brotherly, kind-hearted, and humble in spirit; not returning evil for evil, or insult for insult, but giving a blessing instead."
>
> **I Corinthians 13:8**

Love …

Is patient
Is kind
Is not jealous
Is not a braggart
Is not arrogant
Does not act unbecomingly
Does not seek its own
Is not easily provoked
Keeps no account of wrongs suffered
Does not rejoice in unrighteousness
Rejoices in truth
Bears all things
Believes all things
Hopes all things
Endures all things

As we consider how we are doing at love, each of us, if perfectly honest, would admit to falling short. Our hearts are still marred by selfishness, and we do not love as we should. So where do we begin? If John is right, and *"We love, because He first loved us"* (1 John 4:19), then our loving others begins with our experience of God's love.

APPLY Consider the following exercise and check the appropriate boxes next to the characteristic that best describes your current situation.

My understanding of God's forgiveness of my sins is . . .
- ☐ mostly head knowledge
- ☐ something that grips my heart

My fellowship with God is . . .
- ☐ real and personal
- ☐ rote and impersonal

My confidence that God loves me is based on . . .
- ☐ how well I obey and avoid sin
- ☐ grace and the work of Christ

We need to be awash in the love of God. We need to be confident in His love for us, or we will not be effective at loving others. Summarize by answering the question below:

What does the way I love others say about how I think God loves me?

_____

_____

_____

_____

_____

If we are genuinely experiencing God's love, it will flow through us to others. We may know God loves us but aren't experiencing that love because of sin in our lives that affects our fellowship with God. If this is the case, our lack of experiencing God's love may be affecting how we love others. If you feel this is a problem in your life, take some time to review lesson ten on the "Secret of

"Above all, keep fervent in your love for one another, because love covers a multitude of sins."

I Peter 4:8

"We love, because
He first loved us."

I John 4:19

Power Serving." God wants you to experience His love and forgiveness, and doing so will enable you to love and forgive others. In Revelation 2:4, Jesus warns the church of Ephesus that they had left their *"first love."* They were busy working hard **for** God instead of walking **with** God. He warns that the consequence of not dealing with this issue of pride and self-centeredness is that He would take away their light; in other words, God would no longer shine through them if they didn't return to their first love.

We have the **ability** to love because God loves us. We also have the **responsibility** to love. If we understand the basic teaching of the Bible, we know that we cannot save ourselves. We stand before God always and only by grace and mercy. Yet it is so easy not to be that way with others. On one hand we easily rejoice in mercy and grace from God, yet on the other we often demand justice from each other. We expect others to treat us perfectly, and we get upset when they don't. That isn't love. God has loved us and expects us to love one another unconditionally. In fact, He **commands** us to love one another.

APPLY Have you recently been unloving toward anyone? If so, what steps do you need to take to go and make things right?

_____

_____

_____

_____

_____

What are some ways you can creatively express love to those around you?

_____

_____

_____

_____

Ask God to make you sensitive to the people that make up your world. Pray for them, and ask for ways you can show them love. This is the beginning of ministry. Everyone will recognize you as a disciple of Jesus if you love others. Write out a prayer that expresses this heart in the space below.

_____

_____

_____

_____

_____

_____

_____

_____

_____

We stand before God always and only by grace and mercy. Yet. . . . we often demand justice from each other. We expect others to treat us perfectly, and we get upset when they don't. That isn't love.

The most important thing we are called to do as Christians is to love one another. But since true love (*agapē*) is not just an emotion, but an action, loving one another will result in many practical actions. The Bible lists a great many commands of what God calls us to do for one another. In doing them, we express love.

Each of us has experienced the pain, frustration, and resentment that comes when others fail to live up to our expectations. And yet, often our expectations of ourselves are far less than what we expect of others. Each of the verses on the following page reveals one of the responsibilities that lie on "our side of the fence," for our actions are the only ones we can control.

THE ONE ANOTHER COMMANDS

COMMAND	SCRIPTURE	COMMAND	SCRIPTURE
Not Dealing Falsely	Leviticus 19:11	Accountability	2 Corinthians 9:5
Not Wronging	Leviticus 25:14–17	Meeting Needs	2 Corinthians 11:9
Don't Rule Severely	Leviticus 25:46	Serving Through Love	Galatians 5:13
Pray	1 Samuel 12:23a	Do Not Bite and Devour	Galatians 5:15
Dwell in Unity	Psalm 133:1	Do Not Challenge	Galatians 5:26b
Love at all times	Proverbs 17:17a	Do Not Envy	Galatians 5:26c
Faithful Wounds	Proverbs 27:5–6	Bear Burdens	Galatians 6:2
Sharpen	Proverbs 27:17	Do Good	Galatians 6:10
Lift up	Ecclesiastes 4:9–10	Showing Forbearance	Ephesians 4:2
Do Not Devise Evil	Zechariah 7:10	Speak Truth	Ephesians 4:25
Speak the Truth	Zechariah 8:16	Give, Don't Take	Ephesians 4:27
Be at Peace	Mark 9:50	Be Kind	Ephesians 4:32
Do not seek Glory from Man	John 5:44	Forgive	Ephesians 4:32
Love	John 13:34–35	Be Subject	Ephesians 5:21
Lay Down Your Self	John 15:12–17	Regard Others More Important	Philippians 2:3
Reconcile	Acts 7:26	Do Not Lie	Colossians 3:9
Meet Needs	Acts 11:29	Bearing With	Colossians 3:13
Bring Joy	Acts 15:3	Teaching and Admonishing	Colossians 3:16
Strengthen	Acts 15:32	Abound in Love	1 Thessalonians 3:12
Proclaim the Word	Acts 15:36	Excel in Love	1 Thessalonians 4:9–10
Encourage	Acts 16:40; 18:27	Comfort	1 Thessalonians 4:18
Be Devoted	Romans 12:10a	Encourage and Build Up	1 Thessalonians 5:11
Give Preference	Romans 12:10b	Appreciate and Esteem	1 Thessalonians 5:12–13
Be of One Mind	Romans 12:16	Do Not Repay with Evil	1 Thessalonians 5:15a
Owe Nothing But Love	Romans 13:8	Seek Good	1 Thessalonians 5:15b
Judge Not	Romans 14:13	Give Thanks	2 Thessalonians 1:3
Build Up	Romans 14:19	Point Out	1 Timothy 4:6
Bear Weakness	Romans 15:1–2	No Longer Hateful	Titus 3:1–4
Glorify Together	Romans 15:5–6	Encourage	Hebrews 3:13
Accept One Another	Romans 15:7	Stimulate to Love & Good Deeds	Hebrews 10:24
Admonish	Romans 15:14	Assemble to Encourage	Hebrews 10:25
Do Not Sue	1 Corinthians 6:1–8	Love and Hospitality	Hebrews 13:1–3
Stop Depriving	1 Corinthians 7:5	Visit Widows and Orphans	James 1:27
No Cause for Stumbling	1 Corinthians 8:12	Speak Not Against	James 4:11
Wait	1 Corinthians 11:33	Do Not Complain Against	James 5:9
No Division	1 Corinthians 12:25	Confess	James 5:16a
Respect	1 Corinthians 16:11	Pray	James 5:16b

THE ONE ANOTHER COMMANDS
(CONTINUED)

COMMAND	SCRIPTURE	COMMAND	SCRIPTURE
Love From the Heart	1 Peter 1:22	Laying Down our Lives	1 John 3:14–16
Give a Blessing	1 Peter 3:8–9a	Love in Deed	1 John 3:17–18
Love Fervently	1 Peter 4:8	Believe = Love	1 John 3:23
Hospitality Without Complaint	1 Peter 4:9	Love One Another	1 John 4:7–21
Serve	1 Peter 4:10	Love = Obedience	2 John 1:5
Humility	1 Peter 5:5	Doing for the Brethren	3 John 1:5–6
Walk in the Light	1 John 1:7	Becoming Fellow Workers	3 John 1:7–8
Righteous Love	1 John 3:10–11	Do Good to the Brethren	3 John 1:10–11

Notes

Glossary of Spiritual Gifts

There are four main passages in the New Testament that deal with different types of gifts in the body. Scripture doesn't tell us if these are all the gifts. Instead, the Bible tends to place more emphasis on the categories of gifts and how they function together. A primary Greek term related to spiritual gifts is *charisma* or *charismata*. This isn't a technical term reserved only for spiritual gifts, but simply is a compound Greek word that means "the results of grace" (*charis,* grace, with the suffix *ma*, indicating "the manifested results"). The word is also used for the gift of celibacy, the gift of eternal life, and other gifts. I am not going to attempt to classify the gifts here, but rather, give an explanation of what I believe to be the point of each of the gifts as they appear in the scriptural lists. None of its lists are exhaustive. None of the lists are presented as an end in themselves, but rather, they appear as an illustration of a deeper truth (unity and diversity of the body, structure and operation, etc.). In this glossary I am simply going to take the lists one at a time and try and clarify the gifts listed.

1 CORINTHIANS 12:8–10, 28

Word of Wisdom—The "Word of Wisdom" is the divine enablement to speak practical wisdom to others. It does not refer to intellectual wisdom, but always to practical wisdom, and is accompanied by the ability to live wisely. People with this gift are able to give practical insight into the ways and will of God. They are able to shed light on decisions that were dark and confusing. A biblical example of this gift is James at the Jerusalem counsel in Acts 15.

Word of Knowledge—This refers not to knowledge acquired by study – it's a supernatural endowment. This gift is the ability to make an utterance of knowledge, to speak in such a way as to reveal knowledge that only God could reveal. Some biblical examples of this would be Jesus with the woman at the well in John 4, Peter in Acts 5 with Annanias and Saphira.

I am not going to attempt to clarify the gifts here, but rather, give an explanation of what I believe to be the point of each of the gifts as they appear in the scriptural lists.

Gift of Faith—This does not refer to saving faith or to general faith, but to a special gift—the supernatural ability to trust God and trust Him to accomplish things beyond the normal Christian life—wonder-working faith.

Gifts of Healing—a much-abused gift but a genuine gift nonetheless. It is significant to note that in the Greek, the phrase literally reads "gifts of healings." This seems to suggest that each individual healing is a gift in itself.

Effecting of Miracles—Workings, displays of power (other than healings). The ability to go beyond the laws of nature. A biblical example would be Jesus and Peter walking on the water or Jesus turning water into wine.

Gift of Prophecy—Foretelling (predicting events before they happen) or forthtelling (speaking the mind of God). Even in the Old Testament days, the bulk of a prophet's ministry was forthtelling, pointing out sin and revealing God's perspective. God can choose to operate it the other way, but He usually doesn't.

Distinguishing of Spirits—(Gr. *hermeneutics,* "to discern, to distinguish, to pass judgment") In the early church, as today, Satan sometimes imitates the work of God. Not every miracle is of God; not every prophecy is of God; not every tongue is of God; not every teaching is of God. There are evil spirits working in the world today—this gift is for discerning if a work is of God or not. This is an important gift. It was more necessary before the completion of the Scriptures, but is still needed today.

Various Kinds of Tongues—This is an evangelistic gift, the miraculous and divine ability to speak God's truth to people in a situation where the speaker has no prior knowledge of that language or dialect. See my thoughts on "speaking in tongues" on page 187.

Interpretation of Tongues—The ability of listeners to hear the gospel message in their native language, despite language barriers that may exist between them and the speaker. This gift accompanies the gift of tongues.

(I believe, based on my observances of people in ministry, as well as my study of the instances in Scripture where such gifts are used, that the first nine gifts mentioned in 1 Corinthians 12 are situational gifts—gifts given to an individual in a specific situation to enable them to minister there. If this is true, then it is likely that these gifts are bestowed upon the life of any individual who is surrendered to Christ, and are not therefore, that person's primary gift. Primary gifts, rather, are an abiding enablement, not a situational one.)

Apostles—The divine calling and enablement to plant a church and oversee its development. This gift would likely come with a calling to service in missions or church planting.

Teaching—This gift serves to give instruction; it is the supernatural ability to unfold the Word of God so that people can grasp its meaning. It is not a natural talent, but a spiritual gift. The ability to teach the Word doesn't come from training (seminary) or natural ability, but is a supernatural endowment of both the desire to understand the Word and the ability to communicate it clearly.

Gift of Helps—The supernatural enablement to help in practical ways, using divine energy and motivation. It means to lend a hand, to come to the aid of another. It is perhaps the most needed and most abundant gift in the body.

The Church cannot carry on its task without this gift. All are called to help, but some are uniquely gifted to do it and are given motivation, energy, and enjoyment to be able to fulfill this vital role.

Administrations—The Greek word has the idea of steering or piloting. It is divinely effective at maintaining ongoing functions. This gift is closely related to the gift of leadership in Romans 12, but differs in that Administrations seems aimed at tasks, where Leadership is aimed at people.

ROMANS 12:6–8

Prophecy—The same as listed in 1 Corinthians 12, but in this context, it would seem the "forthtelling" dimension is emphasized. When you look at the Bible as a whole, clearly forthtelling is the primary exercise of prophecy.

Service—Akin to "helps" in 1 Corinthians 12 but differs slightly. The Greek word here is the word "deacon" and has the idea of practical service, waiting on tables. The meaning can and should be interpreted very broadly—any kind of practical service. This gift is ministry to physical needs, not spiritual ones. How do we exercise it? We do so according to the strength God provides (1 Peter 4:11). A biblical example of this gift would be Dorcas of Acts 9:36, 39. It says she was *"abounding in deeds of kindness and charity, which she continually did."* We are told that she made tunics and garments for others.

Teaching—see definition with 1 Corinthians 12.

Exhortation—The Greek word for "exhort" (parakaleo) and "exhortation" (paraklesis) all relate to the action of beseeching or comforting, coming to one's side to help, or acting as an advocate or defender. Perhaps the best synonym for exhortation is encouragement—encouraging people to act on God's Word, encouraging obedience, etc. Prophecy is aimed at the will; whereas, teaching is aimed at the understanding. The ministry of exhortation is aimed at the heart, encouraging the faint-hearted. People blessed with this gift make the best disciplers and the best counselors. By counselors I am not referring to psychologists or psychiatrists who assist people based on secular principles, but those who minister the Word. Exhortation is a Word-based gift.

Giving—The Greek word translated "giving" or "gives" means "to communicate, impart, or share one's own possessions." It is the divine enablement to help financially those in need. Accompanied by discernment, it is the ability to detect needs and discern between true and false needs. This person gives without looking back, without second thoughts, without regret. This doesn't mean that the bearer of this gift must be wealthy, or that those who are wealthy always have this gift. Those who are not blessed with this gift are hardly excused from giving.

Leading—Akin to administrations, the word in this verse translated in the Greek literally means "I stand in front of." Administration involves guiding behind the scenes; leadership is standing out front, being in the public eye or visible. It is the ability to take charge and see that the job gets done. Leaders are good at dividing up tasks between people and following through to make sure tasks get done.

Mercy—The Greek word suggests an inner emotion leading to an outward manifestation of pity. It assumes a need on the part of the recipient and adequate resources on the part of the giver. This ministry involves going to those who need pity, not just resources or money. This is direct personal ministry to those in need—the gift of sympathy. People blessed with this gift are moved to do something about the misery of others—cards, notes, hugs, tears, etc.

EPHESIANS 4:11

Apostles—See definition with 1 Corinthians 12

Prophets—See definition with 1 Corinthians 12

Evangelists—The Greek word literally means "gospelizer" or "good newser." An evangelist is a person who is called and gifted to equip the body to share the good news of the gospel. All Christians are called to share our relationship to God with others. Although those who have had more training, experience, burden, and increased opportunites for obedience may display more fruit than others, this is not saying there is a "gift of evangelism." Unlike the usual operation of this position in the twentieth century, this person's primary ministry is not revivals and evangelistic crusades, but equipping the body to be more effective in sharing Christ (Ephesians 4:12).

Pastors—The term literally means "shepherd" and has the idea of one who nurtures a body of believers much like a shepherd tending to his sheep. This doesn't necessarily mean that all bearing this gift are "pastors" in the vocational sense, but are those who are divinely gifted and burdened to provide pastoral care. It operates sort of as a blending of leading, mercy, and serving. Although it is linked here with teaching, since teaching is isolated elsewhere, it is logical to assume that a person may be gifted to give this kind of care and not be a teacher.

Teachers—See definition with 1 Corinthians 12

1 PETER 4:10–11

Speaking—This would seem to be a general gift category into which we would logically place such gifts as Teaching, Prophecy, Exhortation, and possibly Leading.

Serving—Likewise, this would seem to be another general category into which could be placed gifts such as Service, Mercy and Giving.

OLD TESTAMENT

While most attention is focused only on the gifts mentioned in the New Testament, there are a number of items to be found in the Old Testament that are either identified as gifts or implied as such. As they are pretty much self-explanatory, I have simply listed them with their scriptural references.

Gifts of Music—Singers (1 Chronicles 15:19), instrumentalists (2 Chronicles 34:12), composers (2 Chronicles 29:30), choir directors/conductors (Nehemiah 12:46), music instructors (1 Chronicles 15:22), makers of instruments (2 Chronicles 7:6; 29:26–27).

Gift of Craftsmanship—Exodus 31:3–11

Questions and Answers on Spiritual Gifts

Why Do You Major on the Seven Gifts of Romans 12?

While I have attempted to give you an overview of all four New Testament passages on the subject of spiritual gifts, I have spent more time on the seven we find listed in Romans 12. There are several reasons why I consider this list to be unique. First, though it recognizes the two main divisions we also find in Ephesians 4 and 1 Peter 4, it gives more detail than either of the two latter lists. Secondly, I recognize that it does not give us as exhaustive a treatment of the possibilities as we find in 1 Corinthians. I had to ask myself why. My conclusion is that 1 Corinthians majors on all the different possibilities, while Romans majors on the probabilities. Even the two lists we find in 1 Corinthians 12 are not identical. Thirdly, and most importantly, the church at Rome is the only one of the New Testament churches to receive a letter from Paul that was not founded by any apostle. This explains why the book of Romans is so rich with doctrine. One would expect if the list in 1 Corinthians were all-encompassing gifts of service that each would be repeated in the book of Romans as well. I believe that the gifts of 1 Corinthians are all valid, but some are what I would call "situational" gifts—gifts that God gives to any believer in a certain situation at His own sovereign discretion. Situational gifts are not used on a regular basis. I believe the seven gifts of Romans 12 are the abiding service gifts that we use daily.

The "Cessationist" Debate

One of the issues that always comes up when considering the subject of spiritual gifts is the "Cessationist" debate. One segment of mainstream Christian thought holds the idea that certain spiritual gifts have ceased to exist, while others maintain that all the gifts are active today. The central issue scripturally revolves around the statement of the apostle Paul in 1 Corinthians 13:8—*"but if there are gifts of prophecy, they will be done away; if there are tongues, they will cease; if there is knowledge, it will be done away."* That certain gifts will cease is beyond debate. We have the clear statement of Scripture that some will. The

I believe that the gifts of First Corinthians are all valid, but some are what I would call "situational" gifts— gifts that God gives to any believer in a certain situation at His own sovereign discretion.

question remains, "when will they cease?" I have believers I consider friends on both sides of the issue. In the same way, there are scholars I respect and admire to be found on both sides. Where do I stand personally? I am not a cessationist. I will explain why in a moment, but first let me share some of the arguments in favor of this view. Most cessationists defend their view with 1 Corinthians 13:9–10—*"For we know in part and we prophesy in part; but when the perfect comes, the partial will be done away."* They interpret the phrase *"when the perfect comes"* to refer to the completion of the New Testament canon. In other words, once the New Testament was written, there was no longer a need for the miraculous gifts.

While I would agree with the idea that the New Testament is complete and will not be added to, I do not think that is what Paul is referring to in 1 Corinthians 13. A close examination of the context shows us that as Paul considers the subject, he moves back and forth between the present and the future. In 1 Corinthians 13:12 he writes, *"For now we see in a mirror dimly, but then face to face; now I know in part, but then I will know fully just as I also have been fully known."* The "then" is still future (as is the *"done away"* of verse 10). In verse 12, however, we have more details about this future time. First, Paul tells us that it is not a time of seeing dimly but of seeing *"face to face."* Second, he refers to it as a time of "knowing fully." It would appear that the "perfect" spoken of here as coming refers not to the completion of the canon of Scripture but to when we see Jesus face to face in eternity. Then (and only then) will we know fully (see 1 John 3:1–3).

While I do not see the miraculous gifts as dominating the present age, I cannot confidently say that they no longer exist. At the same time, I do not believe that everything purported to be miraculous actually is or necessarily comes from God. I base my views both on a thorough study of Scripture and my own experiences as a believer which I have tried to interpret through the grid of Scripture. I have personal experience with the miraculous. I make no pretense of being a miracle worker. But I have seen God perform miracles in my life and in those around me. My own salvation was quite a miracle. Overnight, I went from an amoral, athiestic, rebellious drug dealer to a radically-transformed follower of Jesus. It didn't take years of therapy or drug treatment programs. It just took Jesus coming into my life. I have seen miraculous provision of finances for great need. I have seen healed relationships and disasters averted. Perhaps the greatest manifestation of God I have ever witnessed was the inexplicable miracle of God healing my wife from cancer when chemotherapy didn't produce a remission. In 1992, she was diagnosed with a very rare and aggressive form of T-cell Lymphoma, with some twenty tumors scattered in her bones, lymph system, and liver. High doses of chemotherapy left her bald and dangerously immuno-suppressed, but gallium scans revealed they did not leave her cancer-free. Yet just before she was to undergo a bone marrow transplant, God healed her. I'll never forget the conversation I had when the specialist from Vanderbilt University Hospital looked me in the eye and said, "I don't know how to explain it, but I can't find any cancer." That cancer never came back. There was no doubt in our minds that God had worked a miracle—just like the miracle He did at the hands of the apostles in the book of Acts.

What Are Your Thoughts on the Gift of Healing?
I believe the gift of healing functions today, and as I related before, my wife and I speak from personal experience. But I recognize that the gift of healing is much-abused and often misrepresented. Healing is not a person's main gift of service, though some today would claim it so. Peter healed, but that was not his main service to the early church. A study of his life reveals the characteristics of

While I do not see the miraculous gifts as dominating the present age, I cannot confidently say that they no longer exist.

one gifted as a prophet. Paul healed, but his life's work was his gift of teaching. Barnabas healed, but his main gift appears to have been exhortation. When we consider the past and present functioning of this gift, we must acknowledge several important issues. First, not all claims of healing are authentic. There are frauds and charlatans out there. However, the existence of phony healings does not mean that there are no legitimate healings. Second, we must recognize that not all healings or supernatural acts are of God. Scripture tells us that the Anti-Christ will be healed of a fatal wound to the head, but this does not mean it is a work of God. No man can heal at his own will, but only as God allows. I am amazed to see that those who claim the gift of healing often cannot heal themselves of the simplest ailments such as the need for glasses. History is replete with examples of hoaxes and frauds. While I wouldn't put this next example in that category, I did find it quite interesting. Let me share with you an article from my hometown newspaper, the *Chattanooga Times*: The headline reads, "Series Canceled because of Illness." The article goes on to say, "A series of para-liturgical healing and restoration services scheduled this week at four Catholic churches in the Chattanooga area has been canceled because of the illness of the speaker…" (*Chattanooga Times*, September 18, 1990, B-3).

Scripturally, there is no set formula for healing. Some say to heal you must "lay on hands," but it isn't always done that way in the Bible. Sometimes Jesus spoke; sometimes He rubbed mud; sometimes He had them wash in a pool; sometimes He did it long-distance—there was no pat formula, no universal guarantees.

Biblically there are at least four different reasons for sickness:

1) Sometimes sickness comes as a trial (e.g., 2 Corinthians 12, Paul's thorn in the flesh which God did not heal).

2) Sometimes sickness comes as a result of sin (e.g. 1 Corinthians 11 with those abusing the Lord's Supper;; see also James 5:19–20).

3) Sometimes sickness exists for God's glory through its healing (e.g. John 9:3—Jesus healing the man blind from birth; John 11:4—Jesus' healing of Lazarus; Acts 3—Peter healing the man lame from birth, etc.).

4) Sometimes sickness is unto death—to call us home (John 11:4 says that sickness wasn't unto death, indicating some is). I would not want to be healed of my entry into heaven. One important point to mention though in this context is God is able to heal.

What Are Your Thoughts on Speaking in Tongues?

What I say on this subject is sure to hold something to offend almost everyone. Let me say from the outset that I hold my views not from a personal bias or doctrinal agenda. I do not hold my beliefs simply because of what my church or denomination teaches. I have not arrived at my conclusions based merely on my own experiences or lack thereof. I have studied the subject diligently with an open and teachable heart. I have not closed the book or concluded that I have learned all there is to know on the subject, but I have drawn some conclusions that I try to hold honestly before the Lord with an open hand. First, let me share a word of testimony. I became a Christian as a freshman in college through an evangelistic, non-charismatic campus ministry. My conversion was dramatic, as the Lord saved me from an amoral lifestyle of crime, drug abuse, and drug dealing. In those early days of my Christian walk, I tried to get involved in every Christian group and activity on my university campus. I attended meetings with the Baptist Student Union, Campus Crusade for Christ, the Christian Church Fellowship House, the Navigators, the Wesley Foundation, and anything else I could find. I even sang in the Black Student

Association Gospel Choir. (My face was the only white one in the crowd!) My heart was filled with the Lord and open to anything. When I heard of being "baptized with the Holy Ghost" and "speaking in tongues," my attitude was one of wanting anything and everything the Lord had for me. I had charismatic friends who prayed for me and laid hands on me, but I did not have any kind of dramatic experience like they had.

Having studied extensively what the New Testament teaches on the subject, I have drawn a few conclusions. First, a distinction must be made between the gift of speaking in tongues and what is commonly referred to as a "prayer language." What Paul addresses in 1 Corinthians 14 seems to contrast the two. We must begin by acknowledging that a spiritual gift is always defined scripturally as being for the benefit of others. In the words of 1 Corinthians 12:7, we are each given a spiritual gift *"for the common good."* Peter tells us in 1 Peter 4:10 that whatever gift we have, we should *"employ it in serving one another."* What happened at Pentecost certainly seems to fit the parameters of a spiritual gift, but what many call a "prayer language" is exercised for the purpose of personal edification, rather than to minister to others. Second, much of the speaking in tongues practiced in churches today does not respect the limitations the apostle Paul placed on the exercise of this gift—namely, that it only be exercised one person at a time and that it only be used if there is interpretation. Thirdly, Paul indicates that the purpose of the spiritual gift of tongues is as a *"sign for unbelievers"* (1 Corinthians 14:22). In other words, it is an evangelistic gift, not an edification gift. I also believe it to be a situational gift—given not for ongoing use, but given in a particular situation at God's discretion for His sovereign purposes. Notice that at Pentecost *"all"* the believers spoke in tongues, not just a select few. Yet we do not see this group, nor any others who once manifest tongues, mentioned as speaking in tongues again in the book of Acts.

When one considers tongue-speaking in Acts, an important observation is in order. There are only three occurrences recorded in Acts, although I would argue that a fourth is probable. On each occasion, it happens to a different group, and a significant pattern emerges. First, we see the Jewish believers speaking in tongues at Pentecost. Next, we see tongues manifest at the conversion of Cornelius and his household (Acts 10:46). This is the first recorded occasion in Acts where Gentiles became converts. Finally, we see speaking in tongues in Acts 19:6 at the conversion of the disciples of John in Ephesus. The fourth incidence, I would argue, is in Acts 8. This is the record of the first believers among the Samaritans. In this passage, Peter laid hands on them, and they received the Holy Spirit in a manner that was apparently visible, for we are told that Simon *"saw"* that the Spirit was bestowed (Acts 8:18). One of the reasons I believe these Samaritans spoke in tongues is found in Peter's report of the incident when he returns to Jerusalem. He states, *"...the Spirit fell upon them, just as He did upon us at the beginning"* (Acts 11:15). Peter goes on to associate what happened with the promise of John the Baptist regarding being baptized with the Holy Spirit. So what is the pattern here? If you take these four incidents as indicative (which seem to be Luke's intent), you find that speaking in tongues is manifest only when the gospel penetrates each new barrier. First, it appears when Jews who believe in Christ receive the Holy Spirit. Next, it occurs when Samaritans (racially-mixed people with Jewish ancestry) first believe. It occurs once again when Gentiles first believe. Lastly, it occurs in Ephesus, arguably a fulfillment of the *"uttermost parts"* Jesus foretold in Acts 1:8, as those distant from Jerusalem come to full faith in Christ. I believe tongues were manifest at each of these occasions to validate God's working and to affirm to the Jews that others had full standing with God just as they did.

What happened at Pentecost certainly seems to fit the parameters of a spiritual gift, but what many call a "prayer language" is exercised for the purpose of personal edification, rather than to minister to others.

Finally, as I have said before, I am not a "cessationist." I am not able to say with scriptural confidence that the gift of tongues or any of the miraculous gifts have ceased to exist. When Paul states in 1 Corinthians 13:8 that tongues will "cease," the verb is in the middle voice, which when used of persons, indicates intentional, voluntary action upon oneself. When it is used of inanimate objects it indicates reflexive, self-causing action. In other words, the cause of ceasing comes from within. To say it simply, the gift of tongues will eventually work itself out of a job. If tongues are to be seen as an evangelistic gift—a sign to unbelievers (see 1 Corinthians 14:22)—then their primary purpose would seem to be to penetrate new language groups with the gospel. Once there are believers who speak that language, then tongues are no longer needed. Stephen Olford speaks of his father being given the ability to speak a language he had not learned in an evangelistic situation in tribal Africa. I believe God can do that today if He so chooses where it is needed to get the gospel to another language group. Again, I must reiterate, I see that as different from what is called a prayer language or "speaking in tongues."

I hope this explains where I am coming from on the issue of tongues. It is not my desire to be offensive, but rather, to articulate as best I can what I believe. To borrow a phrase from Wayne Grudem's excellent treatment of the subject, I am "open but cautious." I wholeheartedly recommend the book he has edited entitled, *Are Miraculous Gifts for Today?—Four Views* (paperback, 1996, Zondervan). It addresses thoroughly the question, "Are the gifts of tongues, prophecy, and healing for today?" NO, say cessasionists. YES, say Pentecostals and other Christian groups. MAYBE, say a large sector of open-but-cautious evangelicals. What's the answer? Is there an answer? *Are Miraculous Gifts for Today?* takes you to the heart of the charismatic controversy. It provides an impartial format for comparing the four main lines of thinking: Cessationist, Open But Cautious, and Pentecostal/Charismatic. The authors present their positions in an interactive setting that allows for critique, clarification, and defense. This thought-provoking book will help Christians on every side of the miraculous gifts debate to better understand their own position and the positions of others.

If tongues are to be seen as an evangelistic gift—a sign to unbelievers—then their primary purpose would seem to be to penetrate new language groups with the gospel.